The Pull of the Earth

CROSSROADS IN QUALITATIVE INQUIRY

Series Editors
Norman K. Denzin, University of Illinois, Urbana-Champaign
Yvonna S. Lincoln, Texas A&M University

ABOUT THE SERIES

Qualitative methods are material and interpretive practices. They do not stand outside politics and cultural criticism. This spirit of critically imagining and pursuing a more democratic society has been a guiding feature of qualitative inquiry from the very beginning. The Crossroads in Qualitative Inquiry series will take up such methodological and moral issues as the local and the global, text and context, voice, writing for the other, and the presence of the author in the text. The Crossroads series understands that the discourses of a critical, moral methodology are basic to any effort to re-engage the promise of the social sciences for democracy in the 21st Century. This international series creates a space for the exploration of new representational forms and new critical, cultural studies.

SUBMITTING MANUSCRIPTS

Book proposals should be sent to Crossroads in Qualitative Inquiry Series, c/o Norman K. Denzin, Institute for Communication Studies, 810 S. Wright Street, University of Illinois, Champaign, Illinois 61820, or e-mailed to n-denzin@ uiuc.edu.

BOOKS IN THIS SERIES

Incarceration Nation: Investigative Prison Poems of Hope and Terror, by Stephen John Hartnett (2003)

9/11 in American Culture, edited by Norman K. Denzin and Yvonna S. Lincoln (2003)

Turning Points in Qualitative Research: Tying Knots in the Handkerchief, edited by Yvonna S. Lincoln and Norman K. Denzin (2003)

Uprising of Hope: Sharing the Zapatista Journey to Alternative Development, Duncan Earle and Jeanne Simonelli (2005)

Ethnodrama: An Anthology of Reality Theatre, edited by Johnny Saldaña (2005)

Contempt of Court: A Scholar's Battle for Free Speech from Behind Bars, by Rik Scarce (2005)

The Pull of the Earth: Participatory Ethnography in the School Garden, by Laurie Thorp (2006)

Writing in the San/d: Autoethnography among Indigenous Southern Africans, edited by Keyan G. Tomaselli (2006)

The Pull of the Earth

Participatory Ethnography in the School Garden

LAURIE THORP

ALTAMIRA
PRESS

A Division of
ROWMAN & LITTLEFIELD PUBLISHERS, INC.
Lanham • New York • Toronto • Oxford

ALTAMIRA PRESS
A division of Rowman & Littlefield Publishers, Inc.
A wholly owned subsidiary of The Rowman & Littlefield Publishing Group, Inc.
4501 Forbes Boulevard, Suite 200
Lanham, MD 20706
www.altamirapress.com

PO Box 317, Oxford, OX2 9RU, UK

British Library Cataloguing in Publication Information Available

Library of Congress Cataloguing-in-Publication Data

Thorp, Laurie, 1958–
    The pull of the earth : participatory ethnography in the school garden /
Laurie Thorp.
        p. cm. — (Crossroads in qualitative inquiry ; v. 7)
    Includes bibliographical references.
    ISBN 0-7591-0782-3 (cloth : alk. paper) —
    ISBN 0-7591-0783-1 (pbk. : alk. paper)
    1. School gardens—Middle West—Anecdotes. 2. Thorp, Laurie, 1958–
I. Title. II. Series.
    SB55.T56 2006
    372.35'7—dc22   2005021906

Printed in the United States of America

♾™ The paper used in this publication meets the minimum requirements of
American National Standard for Information Sciences—Permanence of Paper
for Printed Library Materials, ANSI/NISO Z39.48-1992.

For the children

Contents

Foreword

H ungry? A short trip to the refrigerator—or, worst case, to the grocery store—will net you fresh fruit, a bakery bagel with cold cream cheese, perhaps some high-energy Trail Mix.

Stressed out by the long hours of work, or the seemingly ceaseless demands of projects, budgets, e-mail at the office? A long weekend in a state or national park, perhaps camping, backpacking, horseback riding, will put things in perspective. A long hike into the gap of an ancient mountain, cooled by the forests and soothed by the rustling of pines and hardwoods, and freshened by the scent of mountain rhododendron, will renew your soul and spirit.

What if neither lovely food nor lovely wilderness were there for you? How would your world be put back together? Where would you find the sustenance, either physical or psychological, to cope with life? Where would you find nourishment and connection?

Laurie Thorp's answer is by no means complete, but it is a good partial answer, and it is an answer now being found in several parts of the country. In a small, semi-rural school serving a high proportion of low-income and poverty-level families and children, a part of the answer came in the form of a garden. Set against the lockstep rhythms of a state-mandated but ill-integrated curriculum structured by high levels of testing and assessment and teacher desperation at the inability to both deliver the curriculum as demanded and simultaneously meet the needs of these children, the story tells how the children of these low-income families struggled daily to make sense of impoverishment and deprivation of many sorts. Mostly, these kids were hungry, and they were, in some sense, rootless. Living in apartments and low-income housing, they had no access to the places of dreaming, the fields of fireflies and flower-strewn meadows, and sun-and-shadow woodlands the author had known as a wandering and imaginative child. Nor did they know the pleasures of a family vegetable and fruit garden, lovingly tended by a "patient elder"—in Thorp's case, her father—where they might learn the mysteries of the seasons, of wooly bears and green tomatoes and earthworms and pill bugs, of sunflowers taller than three young children end on end.

This ethnography is an unsettling mixture of both "difficult knowledge" and "lovely knowledge." It is lovely because it speaks to the awakening of some of the children to the joys and pleasures of fresh food, of making connections between how food is produced, and how it is turned into a delicious and nutritious meal. But it is also difficult because it speaks to other issues, and hints at yet others, way beyond its reach. It speaks to food: why, in a country of so much plenty, children should still go to school hungry, without the means to stroll the seasonal riches so many of us find in local farmers' markets each weekend, or even to get to upscale grocery stores, and so who live on second-rate food—full of fat, salt, and preservatives—because that is what is available, and there is not even a lot of that. It speaks to distribution issues around food, and questions why food distribution systems routinely relegate the poor to lower-quality and "fast" foods, while the middle and upper classes have access to high-quality, nutrient-rich foods, in an astonishing array and variety.

It questions how a state, any state, can create a curriculum and student assessment system so rigid, so inflexible, that actual student needs are rarely met, especially in schools that serve low-income, minority, immigrant, or other children who may need more time, more patience, more individual attention. Thorp asks how schools and state boards of education came to be enemies of teachers, how No Child Left Behind could, in fact, leave both children and teachers behind. Why the endless changes of mandate and curriculum should continually drive good teachers from the classroom. Why teachers should finally give up the fight, and children be left to fend as best they can for themselves. How can a curriculum—the most sophisticated tool of teachers, their bread and butter, to mix metaphors—become an occasion for panic, desperation, fear, alienation? Clearly, something has gone very, very wrong in schools, and we do not know how to fix it.

The story asks us, too, how do the needs of children get met when they need not only teaching, but also nurturing, parenting, being there for them? When children's parents (or other individuals who serve as family members) scrabble day and night to make a living and provide shelter for their children, who will parent them? It is quite clear that the single most important social institution for these children is the school, even if the children move every few months or weeks. It is a constant in their lives and so needs to be staffed with the best, the brightest, the most engaged and caring teachers, who—although it is not a part of their job description—stand for stability, for genuine interest in the children as individuals, who want desperately for them to have a chance at life. And yet it is often those needs which drive the best teachers to seek out other assignments in higher socioeconomic status schools when openings occur. Where do these children find the nurturing and surrogate parenting from the "patient elders" they need during the day?

And finally, we see here a powerful example of participatory research in action. Too few participatory action research projects are written up, and consequently, when students of such approaches look for a variety of examples on which they might model their own work, good exemplary texts are few and far between. The research did not start out being a participatory research project, and Laurie Thorp is honest about that. The confrontation, however, with the backwash of typical research studies—what Shulamit Reinharz terms the "rape model of research" (1979)—drove home the energy drain on teachers' precious time and emotional resources of that approach and drew Laurie Thorp into a different kind of research world. In the research project which eventuated, she found herself working as a "servant-leader" to the needs of teachers and children, the research project redesigned around the needs of children and the creativity of teachers willing to find ways to make literacy, science, biology, mathematics, art, social science, health, and reading grow with and alongside the garden itself. The needs of the Jonesville community, as well as the power of *building* community, came to shape the participation of researcher-teacher and teacher-researchers both.

The community forged gave rise to the only kind of report possible: a multilayered, multivoiced text, with teachers, students, research assistant, and researcher speaking in turn. Thorp, in the best naturalistic and constructivist tradition, acts as orchestrator and midwife to the stories that emanate from the community's work over the years. Consequently, the stories embody many of the experiences: the frustrations of the research assistant. The fears of teachers when new mandates are handed down almost weekly, Orwellian style. The recipes traded among teachers for cooking lessons with the children. Photographs which capture some small part of the wonder and joy of children reconnected to earth, nature, growing things, bugs, worms, and the wonder of harvests, food, and flowers. The drawings of the children. The children's direct, funny, and touching emotions embedded in their garden experiences. And so much more.

A part of the "so much more" is a statement on methodology that Mitch Allen, who gave birth to this series several years ago, calls "the best statement on method I've ever read." Thorp's voice carries all the passion and the power that attends *working with, working alongside, working for* that is participatory action research. It is the voice of community as well as the voice of communion—the shared elation of which George Bernard Shaw speaks: "This is the true joy of life—the being used for a purpose that is recognized by yourself as a mighty one."

Yvonna S. Lincoln
Norman K. Denzin
College Station, Texas
July, 2005

Acknowledgments

Five years ago, the members of my dissertation committee put their loving arms around me and sent me on my way. Encouraged by four strong, wise, and soulful women, I found the courage to take the road less traveled. After the terrible loss of my father, I was tempted to leave the academic life behind: the bottom had dropped out of my world and nothing made sense. However, my committee gently nudged me home saying, "Go, grieve, tend your garden, and then come back and tell us a story." Yvonna Lincoln, Chris Townsend, Carolyn Clark, and Jayne Zajicek, thank you. Thank you for granting me the freedom to grieve, rant, search, experiment, and grow, and ultimately find my way to wholeness again. Throughout that journey, I imagined you as patient midwives assisting in a painful birthing process. It is with a gratefulness that stretches across the sky that I give thanks for the blessing of your friendship and guidance.

Yvonna, I am truly blessed to have you as a mentor. Eight years ago, you encouraged me to write; you sensed I had a wound that wouldn't heal and knew writing would be my remedy. Thank you. More important, thank you for devoting your lifework to critical discourse and scholarship supporting phenomenological interpretivist social science. You have created and legitimized a wide-open space where we may pursue alternative paths of inquiry. Thank you for the years of support you have given to those of us working the margins.

To the teachers, staff, and children of Jonesville Elementary School, thank you for opening your hearts and doors so unreservedly to me. Tending the earth together has truly been one of the great joys of my life. Your spirit of collaboration has demonstrated to me the power of participatory inquiry. But you have been so much more than a "research site." On days when life was too much with me, I would point my car in your direction and lose myself in the garden or see the world anew through the children's eyes. Special thanks to my circle of garden sisters (Carol, Gloria, Sue, Betty, and Kristan). Without you, this project would have been just another school garden: you made it transformational. Strong women all, you are always a source of inspiration. Thank you for your untiring work with those who are most vulnerable in society. May Mother Earth always bless you with blight-free tomatoes.

Heartfelt thanks to Sharon Krinock, Frank Fear, Roberta Miller, The Greater Lansing Food Bank, and Gail Imig of the W. K. Kellogg Foundation for your generous support of Soup From Our Stoop; John Biernbaum for your llama poop (the kids made me say this)—seriously, you are the compost king—and for breathing life into our soil and making fresh greens a reality for these children; Daniel Brooks and Michael Rodriguez for the hours of joy you brought to the garden and into the lives of these children—Thundercakes forever; Emily Reardon for picking up the torch and running with it so effortlessly—you are a gem; Scott Hughes and Nathaniel Freemuth for managing the hundreds of photos, documents, data, and scanned images, and for keeping me organized, thank you; my brother, Jeff Granger—purple hyacinths for you; and finally, Joe, my soul mate, my love, who knows me like no other—thank you for understanding my inner calling and recognizing that I had to answer it. I love every ounce of your being. How lucky I am to grow old with you. I'll meet you in the garden.

Introduction

(or things you should know
before you delve into this story.)

This ethnography is my response to Norman Denzin's (1999, 510) call for an interpretive ethnography that is simultaneously vulnerable and critical, that refuses abstractions and high theory, and seeks to embed the self in storied histories of sacred spaces. Storied histories and sacred spaces. That is the heart of the matter. Who will tell the story of this space? This place. The history unfolding before my eyes is that of the beautiful Earth's demise. A mad unraveling into sameness. Homogenized, bland, and barren landscapes. Sacred? Catch it if you can. Profane places everywhere. The sacred space of my youth—field and forest where I became Daniel Boone—is now a shopping mall: Banana Republic and Starbucks where once stood Sugar Maple and Red Oak. Think about this, we have replaced an expansive place for the imagination with a constructed space for consumption.

How might my story of place contribute insights into our work for a more just and democratic society? I would like to suggest that on this eve of global warming, vanishing species, and code-orange national security (all headlines on the *NBC Nightly News*, January 8, 2004), the single most important act of democracy you can perform is to draw near to the place where you live. Hunker down. Study it. Pay attention. Come to know your place intimately.

Yes, democracy right there under your feet.

Bioregionalists have known this for years. Stephanie Mills says this:

So *"where"* is a critical adverb. Bioregionalism is about a lot of things, but perhaps the most important thing it's about is making one hard choice, which is to answer the question "where?" Where am I going to stay? Where am I going to declare my loyalty? Where am I going to exercise my citizenship? Where is the place I belong? (1991, 41)

These are the questions that pulled me home and propelled my work. Three years ago, I made that one hard choice—I moved back to my hometown and declared: "This is *where* I am going to stay. This is the place where I belong." Until that point in time, "democracy" was a flat and lifeless word, exercised once a year in the voting booth. As Wendell Berry (2001) describes, I, like most Americans, had proxied away my citizenship. In short, I had delegated the practice of democracy to others, namely to the global marketplace. And by mindlessly giving proxy to faraway faceless corporations, we passively participate in the annihilation of our home.

Our planet, our jobs, our health, our children,
our wild places,
sacred spaces are slipping away.
Proxy by proxy.

However, I have written this book not to forecast doom, but rather, to inspire you to ask the same question, "Where am I going to declare my loyalty?" and then to get out there and do it. Once you stake your claim and dig in, this act, this conscious choice, will set off a chain reaction. For me it went something like this: Here is where I'll stay, garden, grieve, garden with schoolchildren, write, witness hunger firsthand, harvest tomatoes with children, eat with children, harvest corn with children, write, cook with children, listen to stories of broken homes and broken lives, grieve, write grants, teach from the garden, become a trusted ally of the school, be outraged at the system, write lesson plans from the garden, attend school board meetings, watch garden expand, outrage at the federal lunch program, audit cafeteria food waste, compost with children, witness the "revolving door of poverty," involve my university students in the garden, write, film, present our work nationally, partner with local food bank, struggle with sustainability . . . radiating outward, burrowing inward. Here is where I exercise my citizenship. Here is where I declare my loyalty. And so the story that fills these pages is the story of how a tiny school-yard garden grew to become a potent site of resistance. Resistance to the homogenization of our land, our food, and our system of education.

You will also find that the *structure* of this book operates as a tool for resistance. Resistance against the master discourse of social science and what counts as an academic text. Heads up, this is a "messy text" (Marcus 1994), this is "experimental writing" (Richardson 1994). As a feminist rebel-child working the margins, I strive to do justice to the cause. I want this text to explore a more fitting way to represent these fields of difference where we do our brand of science. Words alone will never work. Marjorie DeVault (1996) suggests that a feminist methodology should *bring in* what has been ignored, censored, and suppressed by standard research practices. Academic texts have quite effectively ignored, censored, and suppressed all of our senses, all of our being, save the rational mind. It has been a ruthlessly linear, logocentric, masculine read on the world for quite some time. And so this text works to excavate what has been lost—the sensual, visual, emotional, layered, incomplete, excessive data of participatory research. This text is my strategic move, my search for alternatives. The photos, sketches, journal entries, and such are not meant to be cute or to merely provide context. They are the "troubling data" (St. Pierre 1997) that support the knowledge I make. At first glance, the images appear "sunny"; however, take a moment, scratch beneath the surface, and you will likely be troubled.

Elizabeth St. Pierre offers this commentary regarding language under erasure:

> We are very concerned that we have pieces of data, words, to support that knowledge we make. Yet how can language, which regularly falls apart, secure meaning and truth? How can language provide the evidentiary warrant for the production of knowledge in a postmodern world? (1997, 179)

The photographs, sketches, poetry, journal entries, multiple voices, multiple fonts, text play, all work to purposefully complicate the read. "Why all the photos? What's the point?" an editor asks. I counter with, "Why all the *words*? What's the point?" As a woman researcher, words so often fail me. Where I stand, there is so much more than words: there is the sun on your back, the rich smell of earth, muddy shoes, children's giggles, tears, and groans. During those hectic days in the garden, there were long spells of no-words, and yet so much had been spoken. Does this count as data? Somehow it must. Visual artifacts honor the way of knowing that we created. Photos often were our words. Photos did the work of words: they were our memos, our communiqués, passed among research participants;

they spoke volumes; they affirmed. It was our language. It was our cultural stock and trade. "Laurie, I just got a roll of pictures back . . . Did you bring the camera? . . . Our picture was in the paper . . . " Sticky fingerprints and tattered corners vouchsafe rigor in our analysis.

Finally, I recognize language as the ultimate power play and that we cannot make claims of "local" or "place based" while remaining inaccessible with our esoteric language from academia. It is time we come down to earth linguistically and re-inhabit our texts so that our research will also dwell in the terrain of locality. Very early on, it became evident that this must be a polyvocal text. Participatory research has that effect, you know; the multiple voices in this text are integral to our sustained sense of community; anything less would be a violation of our commitment to one another. My responsibility in this project became quite clear: turn up the volume on this glorious chorus of voices from the garden. In a system where it is mighty difficult to be heard, I can help to get the word out; I can carry the message across the border. The voices take the form of children's garden chatter, journal entries, teacher talk over late-night beers, photo elicitation, pickle recipes, retrospective fieldnotes, and poetry to name just a few. And so this "academic text" is a continuation of my quest to transgress authoritarian knowledge production. I take my cue from Patti Lather (1993) who advocates a "less comfortable" social science as a counterbalance to scientific certainty and conformity. As an agriculturist, I move strategically into the less-comfortable spaces of subjectivity, messy qualitative data, contradictory interpretations and values. You may find the chapters that follow will interrupt one another. It may not be a smooth or comfortable read. Bump. An excessive profusion of ideas. This is feminist writing in a pounding storm. For there is no making sense of something as complicated and absurd as children going hungry in a time of epidemic obesity. There is no making sense of something as outrageous as vanishing species in a time of eighty-nine-billion-dollar defense spending.

Nature writer David James Duncan (2000) reminds us that when the place you inhabit is threatened, your deep animal instinct is to respond with frenzy. Observe the thrashing wings and wild strafing of a mother cardinal when her nest and fledglings are approached. Frenzy. This book is my frenzied response to the destruction of the people and places I love. How to remain calm when so much is at stake? What you will find is a frantic, emotional SOS, a wing-flapping-plea-in-the-name-of-our-common-humanity book. A woman-full, emotion-rich clarion call to our senses: sight (sunflower golden yellow), sound (cacophony of children's voices), smell (tomato foliage in the summer sun), touch (newly tilled warm soil after so many months of winter), and "Mrs. Thorp, the wheat is up!" book.

As children become cut off from nature, our story of the universe or worldview has become increasingly individuated and lifeless. Numerous authors (see for example, Shepard 1977, Swimme 1996, Sheldrake and Fox 1996) attribute this dysfunctional cosmology for most of our contemporary problems. Strip malls and urban blight are what greet our children today. I think we can do better. Doing better, yes; as a pressing matter of social justice, however, at this moment in our planetary history, it may be a matter of survival. Many scientists agree that all of our big-ticket items—air, water, soil—are at serious risk. The clock is ticking and as Stephen J. Gould says (1991, 14), "We cannot win this battle to save species and environments without forging an emotional bond between ourselves and nature as well, for we will not fight to save what we do not love."

Chapters one to four are my dirt-under-the-fingernails account of the forging of these bonds. It is a story about love and connection, reciprocity and time. Our school-yard garden is a place of connection because it operates according to rhythms that differ from the clipped pace of public education. The larger rhythms in a garden cannot be segmented, fragmented, or dissociated. You cannot hurry a garden; it is beholden to a temporal cadence unaffected by human clocks and schedules. Stepping out of the classroom and into the garden, one enters a place of slow rhythmic continuity. How often have I had to return a child to the classroom with such apologies as "Sorry we just lost track of time"? Clock time drops away and children are able to experience the living cycles of nature. Students have come to depend on the continuity of the garden, and that's a good sign. In the three years I have been at this school, we have lived through a succession of five principals. Very little here the children can depend on. But sure as spring follows winter, the garden will be here. Promise.

Tragically, as we scramble to secure any parcel of green for our children, vast tracts of nature are paved over and destroyed by unrestrained development in the rampant commercialization of our planet. Five acres per hour here in Michigan. Five acres per hour. Already, half of our wetlands have been destroyed. Between 1982 and 1992, over twelve thousand farms were lost. A runaway train this. As I come to understand the lives of the children in this study, I see myriad additional threats to their connection with nature: the flight and mobility associated with poverty, the seduction of technology, overloaded curricular pacing guides, latchkey lives lived behind locked doors to name a few. Like sailors returning from months at sea, our children come to us increasingly in a state of sensory deprivation. As one teacher in this study pleaded, "They are starved for experience." This is especially true for socially disadvantaged children: they do not have opportunities to *experience* the diversity and reciprocity of nature afforded to children of privilege. The garden is our attempt to reverse this injustice. But you need not take my word on this: Chapter five was crafted entirely by the students of Jonesville Elementary School. In this chapter, children share their thoughts and feelings about the garden through prose, poetry, artwork, and journal entries.

For children in poverty, I have found it is a double dose of deprivation. Held hostage by the National School Lunch Program, or free and reduced-price lunches, these children are condemned to a diet of highly processed fast food. Trucked-in and plastic-wrapped, food is offered as a mere commodity for consumption. Whole food or slow food is a social good afforded only to those of privilege. What we are witnessing is nothing short of food totalitarianism. Governed by giant institutions (such as the U.S. Departments of Education and Agriculture to name two), the food served in the cafeteria of this school has lost its cultural and communal dimension. One size fits all—especially if you are poor and voiceless. Woven throughout each chapter you will hear stories of how we are attempting to reconnect children to food and food to place. Chapter six, written by Kristan Small, fourth grade teacher at Jonesville School, provides insights into the complexities of mandated curriculum pitted against our vegetable garden. No easy answers here. In chapter seven, Daniel Brooks, a university student volunteer at Jonesville School, chronicles his year spent eating the federal lunches and gardening with the children. Daniel became a trusted ally of the children and teachers, but in addition, he did ethnography in the "spaces" where I didn't fit. As a student, Daniel was able to hang out with the children and teachers in a context entirely different from what I could ever hope for as a university researcher.

In an effort to chase assessment numbers, curricular change is a constant in this school district. Central to the machinations of efficient schooling is the subordination of teachers to an institutional ethic of control and accountability. "We take an oath to uphold the state curriculum," Betty earnestly tells me. She continues, "Assessment drives your practice." Under this heavy yoke of mandated curriculum and continual assessment, I have found that the garden satisfies the teachers' contained urge to create connections across the curriculum—to make whole again a body of knowledge that has been artificially subdivided into tidy categories. Teachers have begun to craft their own individualized garden curriculum: "We enjoy the creativity of asking: How can growing pumpkins be a literacy activity?" At the same time, I hear, "The garden is upsetting to me, upsetting because we are torn between what we know is good and right for the children, for ourselves, and for the planet and what is rewarded in the system."

Grounded in three years of ethnographic inquiry, this study represents what it means for me to become a participatory researcher. Located just ten miles from a tier-one, research-intensive university, the schools in this district are heavily utilized for academic study; cynicism regarding academic research runs high among teachers. My first few months on site were spent proving to the teachers that I wasn't going to take what I needed and leave. Not a chance. Enter 250 sweaty-palmed little ones aching for their time in the warm May sun—all experiencing the pull of the earth. Chapter eight is my solemn testimony on behalf of every participatory method in the researcher's toolbox. In this chapter, I suggest that we must let loose the reins of our research and try with all our might to understand the pressing questions of those we study. Then roll up our sleeves, grab a hoe, and get to work.

Paul Shepard (1977) in his brilliant essay "Place in American Culture" argues that children must have ample opportunities for direct experience with the natural world. Without this period of "imprinting" on a diverse landscape, he posits, we fail to develop fully as human beings. He suggests that our wholesale destruction of wild landscapes has grave consequences not only for our biosphere but also for our selfhood. In chapter nine, my closing chapter, I tell the story of Thomas, illustrating Shepard's thesis and pointing to the healing powers of nature. The parable of Thomas is emblematic of nearly all of our children in poverty; we often enumerate the deficiencies associated with the poor to include adequate housing, food, and health care; however, seldom do we mention access to the natural world. In this chapter, I close with the question, What endures? As a framework for conclusions and recommendations, this question continues to plague me as I search for solid ground in the chaos of public schooling and environmental degradation.

Recently while eating lunch with the teachers, I heard, "Yesterday I asked my kids to draw where they play outside. Know what? Most couldn't do it. They don't go outside. Where would they go? Into the streets?"

How to remain calm when so much is at stake?
And so we garden.

Laurie Thorp
East Lansing, Michigan

CHAPTER

ONE

Locating the author,
locating the other.

I write to record what I love in the face of loss.

—Terry Tempest Williams,
Red: Passion and Patience in the Desert

I could tell you the foundation of this study is firmly rooted in the work of my predecessors, but that would be a lie. I could coax you into this book with alarming statistics of educational decline and ecological degradation, but that is a tired and worn-out journalistic tactic. I could wave the banner of some large and lasting purpose, but whom are we kidding? Still I dance around the deeper issues. As a fledgling qualitative researcher, this is my first bold step into the constructivist epistemology that I call home. I am shedding the too-tight shoe of positivist science, and that feels good. However liberating, this coming out also feels risky and vulnerable. The tables are turned. As Ruth Behar reveals our position in traditional inquiry (1993, 273), "We ask for revelations from others, but reveal little or nothing of ourselves; we make others vulnerable, but we ourselves remain invulnerable." The disembodied voice from nowhere ceases to be an option in this "seventh moment" of qualitative research. Poststructuralism demands that researchers as writers reveal their collusions in the texts they create. Come out, come out, wherever you are. Laurel Richardson (1994) directs us as qualitative writers to understand ourselves as persons writing from particular positions at specific times.

That specific time began in early April 1999. I can remember the precise moment it happened. The very second when the gossamer silk threads of that entangled web called family pulled my very being into this journey. It was a pull so strong and so deep in my soul that it hurt. It was a powerful hurt. The kind of blow-to-the-belly hurt that only love can render. I stood there watching my brother deliver a final rite of spring so lovingly and so tenderly that, in one brief moment, it wiped the slate clean. The chasm of distance that once stood between us was gone, all because of that hyacinth. That exquisite little hyacinth—I can see it all as if it were yesterday. He pulled it out from under his jacket and there it was: a purple hyacinth, freshly cut from Dad's garden, sealed in a Ziploc bag. Yes, a Ziploc bag with his precious offering of love and life inside. You see, he had to smuggle this breath of spring into the cardiac care unit because the rules read: "Fresh flowers not allowed in CCU." (Go figure that stroke of institutional genius; you're dying and they won't allow you this one last pleasure.) His offering required no explanation; we both knew what it represented. Dad was always happiest in his garden: this was his greatest joy, the artist's palette, his hedge against famine and church, all rolled up in one. So there we were, our little family, just the three of us, huddled amid the IV drips and heaving ventilator, rhythmically heaving, heaving, heaving, slow laborious contractions bringing forth a new life. And there we stood clinging to the life energy of a purple hyacinth in a Ziploc bag.

As Richardson (1994) describes, this is writing as inquiry: inquiry into my deep, abiding connection to the earth, and inquiry into many children's tenuous, new connections to a school-yard plot of soil. And somehow, these stories will be stitched together into a meaningful whole. I plunge ahead faithfully with these bright and shiny new tools of the trade. It is an emergent phenomenon; this I do believe. This is inquiry as *bricolage*; Norman Denzin and Yvonna Lincoln beautifully describe:

> The *bricoleur* understands that research is an interactive process shaped by his or her personal history, biography, gender, social class, race, and ethnicity, and those of the people in the setting. The *bricoleur* knows that science is power, for all research findings have political implications. There is no value-free science. The *bricoleur* also knows that researchers tell stories about the worlds they have studied. (1998, 4)

So dear reader, I offer you a story, a love story actually. I fully recognize how irreconcilable this mixing of science and love may appear. My colleagues on the other side of the fence may well declare subjectivity and contamination. That is the worn-out battlefield where *social* meets *science*. But I am not a warrior; I am a gardener with a story to tell and some healing to do. And, as I look around me, I see that *we are all wounded*; we are all in need of a little healing. The stories jump out at me so fast and furious, I doubt my ability to capture them all—to get it right. I lay down the words in fits and jerks not knowing where they lead nor understanding their pattern. Yet I know from my own experience that it is in the telling and retelling of these stories that our wounds can heal and some sense can be made of it all. My head is swimming with voices: wounded teachers, wounded children, wounded families, wounded storyteller. I offer this tiny plot of land, carved out of a school yard, as a venue for healing, learning, and love. Faithfully we sow our seeds of hope and wait for the unfolding answer. Heaving, heaving, heaving, we *all* cling to life support, and the room feels so crowded.

locating the other.

This is a story about moments of becoming, wonder, and connection at a small elementary school in the Midwest. Traveling the rural roads out to Jonesville Elementary School for my very first visit, I am struck by the pastoral beauty of the farmland that surrounds the school. Strip malls and commercial enterprises of the city give way to tidy homesteads, cornfields, and wide-open vistas. Paradoxically though, the children of this school are not farm children. This district "outpost" (a term frequently used to describe Jonesville School) serves three decidedly urban neighborhoods in the surrounding community. Children are bused in from the inner city and two low-income mobile-home neighborhoods. I am told this is a throwback from the desegregation orders of the seventies, which somehow never went away. As a result, the school population is an ethnically diverse mix of African American, Hispanic, Asian, Arab, and Native American. District-wide, over forty languages and dialects are spoken. Teachers proudly tell me, "This is our strength," and it truly is one of their many strengths. Yet this glorious strength comes at a mighty price for these are the faces of poverty: 58 percent of the 260 students are on the federal free and reduced-lunches program. This number as I have come to find out is a powerful number in the education business. Kristan Small, one of my key informants, looked me dead in the eye and said, "That number is very telling you know." I shake my head: no, I don't know. "Alfie Kohn (a noted educational researcher) can look at that number and tell you within a few percentage points what your standardized assessment scores will be. There is a direct correlation between privilege and test scores." "So why bother," I wonder aloud marveling at teachers' perseverance to perform against losing odds. "Right," Kristan agreed. "Why bother? And here is the kicker. Kohn admonishes us as teachers *not* to try and beat these odds because he says, if we do happen to pull our scores up slightly, that means we are teaching to the test, and deep, meaningful learning has been abandoned."

And yet after only a few days at the school, I saw that the deep, meaningful learning had *definitely not* been abandoned by these dedicated and caring educators. In fact, Jonesville School prides itself in its unique educational philosophy within the district. Jonesville teachers have made a commitment to a multiage or "streaming" approach to learning. Children are grouped in multiage settings such as K-1, 2-3, and so on, shifting the focus away from annual promotion to each child's unique readiness. This was a grassroots movement brought forth by the teachers, not mandated or imposed externally. There is an ethos of student-centered learning that pervades throughout the building. Classrooms are rich with literature, artwork, colorful manipulatives, plants, animals, beanbag chairs, and posters of positive reinforcement. Sadly, though, bubbling just below the surface of this marvelous environment of caring, I see and hear strains of fear and anger at the system.

change is the only constant.

My first glimpse into the depths of fear and frustration came with an invitation from Kristan to attend a faculty meeting scheduled to garner input for the district concerning curricular reform. This meeting in and of itself spoke volumes about the relationship between faculty and central administration; Kristan, as a liaison between "downtown" and Jonesville School, was asked to solicit feedback for curricular change because of a lack of response from a recent survey attempt by the district. This survey requesting suggestions for curricular change had an abysmal return rate of less than 5 percent. Noting my amazement, Kristan commented, "There is a huge disconnect between us and them." As I listened to the meeting unfold, the reasons for this disconnect became clear. Kristan opened the meeting by sharing with her colleagues what she had learned in the last few months "downtown." The latest movement afoot from administration was a push for "real-time student assessment." An annual assessment it seems was no longer enough. Reacting to the "huge constituent unrest," administrators felt the need to count and measure more. Conveying this push for assessment, Kristan boldly states, "We can't wait until fourth grade." I should note that underscoring this reference to constituent unrest was the looming state school voucher proposal being brought before the voters later that year. Here was a meeting, called for the purpose of gathering information to improve a curriculum, being sidetracked right from the start by even greater issues of bureaucratic scrutiny and distrust. Although this initiative was being sold under the guise of student assessment, the teachers immediately cried foul and interpreted this as one more way of forcing teacher accountability, one more brick in the wall of fear and distrust.

Allowing this discussion to run its course, the conversation finally came back to curriculum revision. I am informed that the core curriculum (language arts, mathematics, science, and social studies) is a state document that is district aligned. Further complicating this situation are the politics surrounding site-based management that came into vogue with the previous Democratic governor but has since lost support from the current Republican governor and legislators in power. There once was great latitude for even greater local adjustments of the state curriculum (a state law is still on the books to support this), but the political climate has dramatically eroded enthusiasm for this. Now it appears that there is nothing but cynicism for "the framework"—another term used to refer to this ever-changing document. One teacher emphatically states, "We have been working without a reliable curriculum for ten years." Another teacher counters, "We have a good curriculum, but we are ill prepared. We need professional development." "If you can't provide me with the resources, don't expect me to teach it!" a voice shouts from across the room. A lower elementary schoolteacher moans, "There is way too much science!" Kristan looks at me and winks. "By the fourth grade, all human knowledge is supposed to be covered." Later, Kristan reassures this teacher that the science curriculum has been officially "tossed." Surprisingly, this provides no relief to the teacher's angst; in fact, it provokes even greater dismay at "downtown." Betty, a seasoned veteran of twenty-two years in the district, mutters under her breath to me, "Mandates and change, we are faced with this constantly. Eventually, I don't know, three years, five years, ten years down the road, you just shut down and you go back to your room, close the door, and teach from the basal." Overhearing this comment, Gloria, a lower elementary teacher, leans forward and tells me that their union is writing a response to district change. When I ask what that means, I am told that the union has become concerned by the rate of change and wants to ensure that all curricular changes are "thoughtful." Distracting me from this obtuse explanation, a teacher asks about the status of their "pacing guide." Unfamiliar with yet another term, I am told that the pacing guide is an attempt by the district to take "all of human knowledge" and structure it into a forty-week school calendar. "We aren't concerned with what is right! We should set our pace according to our children! The official pace is being told to us," the teacher adds. Kristan explains to me that it has been determined that there is the equivalent of eighty-four weeks worth of lessons in the current state curriculum. This astounding information was calculated by the district during one of their past *three* attempts at completing this impossible task. After absorbing what I heard at this meeting, it became crystal clear to me why there was so little interest in my offer of a newly authored garden-based curriculum.

our product is our test scores.

During subsequent meetings and conversations with teachers and the school principal, the complexity of this school culture was spelled out for me in greater detail. Central to the machinations of efficient schooling is the subordination of these women by an institutional ethic of control and accountability. As Kristan explained to me, the superintendent uses a "corporate model" for the district. "Accountability is *big*; our product is our test scores." As she clarifies this for me, I sense how conflicted she feels about the values that surround these issues. Kristan clearly respects the new superintendent, yet there is hesitation in her support for the numbers game. Kristan is a learned woman in educational theory and understands that bigger questions of authentic learning and professional discourse have been stifled. Yet she proceeds on with her elucidation of the drive for numbers, "You see, the district wants to align the budget with real-time assessment; it needs to be data-driven. For example, if there are low scores on the concept of motion then provide budget dollars for professional development on motion." When I ask her about the possibility of entertaining alternative forms of assessment, she quickly replies, "The district needs numbers to crunch; it will not fund or support an assessment that is not quantitative. Qualitative assessment is too expensive and time consuming." I tell Kristan that I knew the push for teacher accountability was bad but that I had no idea it was this oppressive. "And now there is talk downtown of the MAT [Metropolitan Achievement

Test] for every grade level." Begrudgingly she concedes, "Assessment informs and drives your practice."

don't get lost in the numbers.

Playing the numbers game is a constant balancing act for Dee, the principal of Jonesville School. Hanging over her head like a guillotine is the label of "underperforming school." When I asked her about this label, she simply pointed to the Jonesville School Success Card (prominently posted on the office wall), which is compiled by the district every school year. The "success card" summarizes the school's performance on the state's standardized assessment program against the school board's goals. At a glance, one could quickly see that Jonesville School was indeed "underperforming" in all four core curriculum categories. I later learned that sixteen out of the thirty-one schools in the district fell into this category of "underperforming" or "loser school." Amazingly, Dee remains a powerhouse of positive energy, leading her teachers through the oppressive atmosphere of threatened school closure, shrinking budgets, and increased pressure for "success." At a faculty meeting in December, I witnessed Dee begin to rally her troops in preparation for the upcoming annual assessment onslaught in late January. "Don't get caught up in the board's goals. Look at personal effectiveness. What will be effective for you? State your goals and check *your* data. How can you become an effective practitioner? I'm asking you to be reflective, cognizant of what you are doing." It didn't dawn on me until months later, when I was interpreting this data, that Dee was in essence espousing a philosophy of action research at this meeting. She continued, "Teachers, be reflective: Ask yourselves if what you are teaching is making a difference. Are you moving your objectives forward? How do *you* assess your teaching? Don't get lost in the numbers." I left that meeting with a deep abiding respect for this one-woman warrior in the battle against a system of evaluation based solely on numbers. Empowering teachers to engage in self-reflective practice under the heavy hand of routine standardized assessment and the moving target of curricular change will be a challenge, to say the least. Everywhere I look, I see the strain created by an organizational system designed for standardized, normative outcomes. Julie, an upper elementary schoolteacher summed up the demoralizing effect this push for numbers has had on teachers. Visibly worn-out, she grabbed me in the hallway one afternoon and talked a steady stream, focusing on the call for increased teacher accountability at both the state and national levels: "I don't know how much more dehumanizing it can get."

everyone has promises.

For the teachers of Jonesville School, attempts at educational intervention and inquiry are often dehumanizing. As an "underperforming school," Jonesville is no stranger to the myriad interventions available in educational reform. During a dinner conversation with Kristan one evening, I learned of the district's past efforts at dealing with persistent problems in education. She recounted, "We once had 'focus schools' designed to attract and retain students based on a particular strength of the building, but that is gone now; alternatively, schools threatened with closure were *told* to apply to become magnet schools, but this doesn't work because our union doesn't allow an entire building to be cleared out." Upon my prompting for clarification, Kristan explained that prior to the union response to focus or magnet schools, the process of creating these schools clearly identified "good teachers" and "bad teachers" in a building, which was very destructive to school community. In Kristan's opinion, magnet and focus schools were also detrimental to the fabric of neighborhood communities, often encouraging families to abandon their neighborhood school for "something better" elsewhere. With this manipulation of the component parts by an external authority, deep systemic problems remained unaddressed and local stakeholders remain powerless.

    A vivid example of an intervention violating local knowledge and expertise occurred several months prior to the annual state assessment at Jonesville School. I arrived at the school early one October morning (assessments take place in late January), to find several teachers in the hallway angrily discussing a memo they had received from downtown informing them that a psychologist contracted by the district would be working with their students in preparation for the state testing. The teachers were outraged. How could an outsider brought in for ten weeks understand their students better than they did? One particularly enraged teacher declared that she had known the families of most of her students for years and understood intimately the dynamics in these children's lives. Another teacher stated that removing a child from much-needed classroom instruction for counseling with a stranger was clearly not going to improve test performance. Blatantly ignoring the wealth of local knowledge and failing to involve the teachers in this decision, the district administrators had made a bad situation worse. Instead of easing tension about assessments, the downtown authority had in fact increased it. Everyone has promises; few seem to deliver.

    Promises can also come from within the school community. External authorities are not alone in this quest for the silver bullet. Construct a culture based on numeric performance and before you know it, everyone is chasing numbers. One day during recess duty, Betty expressed to me her resentment toward a teacher, nodding in the woman's direction, "She thinks she is going to save our school." I sensed that the external pressure to perform was closing this culture in on itself, causing teachers to feel increasingly defensive. Later that afternoon when I asked Kristan to reflect on this theory, she replied in her usual rapid-fire way, "Do you know that we currently have a *three-year* attrition rate!" I asked her why she thought this was occurring. "It's due to isolation, to the increasing needs of our children, to state and district demands . . . " her voice trailed off as she wearily gazed at the chaos of the classroom, landing her focus on the mounds of paper on her desk as if to say, "Would you last three years at this?" Knowing my personal history (I had only lasted four years in elementary education), she surmised the answer, no, I wouldn't last.

they almost always know what they want to know.

So how could I avoid being just another empty promise? Situated ten miles from a tier-one university, Jonesville, along with the other schools in the district, is regularly used as a site for academic research. Late in September, I had the good fortune to witness a typical research relationship with the local schools. Gloria, who would become another key informant, invited me one afternoon to attend a meeting with a researcher from the university who was interested in studying how teachers plan. The reason Gloria wanted to include me was that she thought she could kill two birds with one stone: she wanted to start writing up all the "great" lessons that were emerging from the garden *and* she could use these lessons to participate in the other study. I was thrilled. Not only had Gloria initiated the idea of writing up garden lessons but also she was granting me entrée into this "other" world of research. As I reflect back on this moment, it was a turning point in my research at Jonesville School; it was a moment of grace. This gift of affirmation from Gloria set my research on an entirely new trajectory; there was a paradigmatic shift that week from *my* research to *our* collaborative work. There was a letting go of the reins of control, which was incredibly liberating and reassuring. All self-doubt concerning my role in this project faded away with this *validation*. The study had been deemed trustworthy enough to act upon—"let's write up these great lessons." This conversation also represented the validation of voice. Gloria was attempting to communicate meaning to her colleagues and me in a teacher's most familiar written genre—the lesson plan.

One week later, I arrived in Gloria's room at 4:00 p.m. to sit in on the meeting for this new study that Gloria and her teaching partner, Carol, were about to begin. While waiting for the arrival of the university researcher, we sat together on pint-size chairs and planned the logistics for our upcoming salsa-making festival with their students. Finally, thirty minutes late and flustered, the researcher rushed in the door muttering something about getting lost; she was introduced as Sandy. Sandy then spent the next few minutes fumbling around setting up and testing her audio-taping apparatus. The worn-out, overscheduled teachers had now spent forty minutes of their precious time waiting for this meeting to begin. Sandy proceeded to tell these veteran teachers what a "good" lesson plan

entails. I silently wondered how this could be an inquiry into how teachers plan? Sandy handed Gloria and Carol a two-page typed guide to lesson planning, which she wanted them to follow for the *ten* lesson plans they were requested to produce. I listened with feelings of anger and embarrassment: anger at the researcher's insensitivity to local knowledge and embarrassed at this representation of the academy's dismal relationship with society.

The conversation that ensued following our meeting with Sandy was a critical point of departure in my development as a researcher. Our conversation also marked that wondrous moment in participatory research when the lines between researcher and researched begin to blur, when relationships solidify and new voices emerge. Unable to withhold my comments any longer, I blurted out, "I am appalled at what I just witnessed. How can this be a study of how teachers plan when she has told you exactly how to plan?" I continued to bluster and huff about the glaring methodological gaps in Sandy's study, when Carol in her usual calm and steady voice interrupted me and said, "Yes, they almost always know what they want to know. Most academic research is curiosity taken to the extreme perversion of idiocy." From that moment forward, my commitment was to developing sensitivity to local knowledge, to staying open to an emergent process. Gloria added that this project with Sandy was pretty typical their experiences with academic research, then added, "You are very atypical." How would I continue to demonstrate to these women that indeed, I was not like the other researchers? How would I demonstrate that I was committed to a different kind of research? The answer was quite simple; it was what I was brought home to do. I must garden.

T W O

The grace of a garden.

Until we feel graced we are not in a position
to deal with our wounds.

—Matthew Fox, *Natural Grace*

*Fieldnote (9 Sep 2000): We had the kids come to the back table
to work with me chopping vegetables (from the garden) for salsa.
They all were so curious, most didn't want to go back to their seats.
The most rewarding moment today was when James came running
back into the room while waiting for his bus and asked me if he
could take some of the salsa home.*

I have thought long and hard about this encounter and have tried to
capture what happened in a word or two: pride, accomplishment,
success. But these words are all too feeble. Now, it is quite clear that
what happened that day for both James and me was grace. It was pride,
accomplishment, and thanks, all rolled up into one. All our hard work
together—digging, hoeing, watering, weeding—had culminated in this
moment of grace.

Let me explain. To say that Jonesville Elementary School was badly in
need of something to crow about, to find a point of pride was a start. But
I am now convinced that pride was only half of the story. The garden created a space amid the turmoil and scrutiny of schooling for us to feel

graced. Wounded as we all were, there was a reason, finally, to give thanks: a moment's reprieve. I present this interpretation early in my story because I think this state of gratefulness was a critical element to the foundation for the success of the garden. The teachers, staff, and children were able to view their world through a new lens because of the garden. They were able to feel blessed rather than cursed.

> *Fieldnote (23 May 2000): Betty told me today that last year the garden didn't get planted until the last day of school (mid-June) and that she did it all by herself, frantically shoving plants in the ground. She said that eventually it turned into their "prairie ecosystem."*

And of course, the growth of the garden was grace in my own life. This idea to come home and garden through my grief with 250 children was not so crazy after all.

> *Fieldnote (19 July 2000): Went with Betty to weed and water the garden this morning. The garden is doing really well. Still no diseases or bug problems, such a relief. And people had such concerns about summer maintenance.*

By mid-July, I was able to breathe a sigh of relief: the garden was not merely surviving; it was flourishing. Fear and worry gave way to grace and

wonder. By late August and the advent of school, the garden had exploded into a cornucopia of flowers and vegetables.

The garden was bursting at the seams and so were we with pride in our accomplishment: this year there was a garden instead of a prairie. Faculty and staff all agreed that we needed to contact the local newspaper and share our accomplishment with the world.

After a phone call arranging for a reporter and photographer to visit Jonesville School, an interesting thing happened: students and teachers all started to talk about the "story" they wanted to tell the newspaper. I hadn't anticipated this. But of course, there was finally some good news to share. Did they want to tell the newspaper about our amazing crop of tomatoes and our homemade salsa? Did they want to tell about the biggest pumpkin ever or our sunflower jungle? How about the popcorn? As an ethnographer, I anticipated this story within the story. What

would they consider to be important in the telling of the garden story? Right on cue, their answer emerged from the garden. By this time, the second week in September, our turnip crop was shouting to be pulled from the ground. These were no ordinary turnips, mind you; these were "great, big, giant, enormous turnips." While weeding one afternoon, Carol told me about a children's book written about a great, big, giant, enormous turnip. It is a story of teamwork, cooperation, and communal nourishment centered around the harvest of a giant turnip from a farmer's field. *This* was the story Jonesville School wanted to tell. They wanted to tell the story of their newly found sense of community.

At the appointed hour, we all lined up (hands on waists

just as in the story) and *together*, we pulled our giant turnip—POP, click—for the reporter and photographer.

voices from the garden.

William Pinar says voice is meaning that resides in the individual and enables that individual to participate in community. The struggle for voice begins when a person attempts to communicate meaning to someone else. Finding the words, speaking for oneself, and being heard are all part of this communal process.

> *Fieldnote (11 Sep 2000): Went out to school to meet the reporter. It went really well. I was able to have her talk with Dee, Kristan, Betty, Sue, and Sally, and she interviewed even little James. I am so relieved, I want this to be their story, not mine.*

The amazing growth of a fifty-nine-cent packet of turnip seeds had empowered these teachers and children to have a voice in a system where it is mighty difficult to be heard.

> *Fieldnote (13 Sep 2000): Back out to the school today to sense the reaction of our newspaper article. I walked into the office just when Dee (principal) was reading it. She kept repeating, "This is awesome, this is awesome. This will be so good for us." Walked into Carol's class and they had already laminated it and put it up on their bulletin board. James (who was quoted in the article) found me and gave me a high-five.*

I have been told by numerous teachers that Sue is the most stunning example of empowerment and finding her voice as a result of the garden. "She is a completely different person this year; she is transformed," Kristan informed me. I first became aware of Sue's voice through little notes, grant applications, and magazine articles left in my mailbox at school. Like a message in a bottle, I would find such notes as:

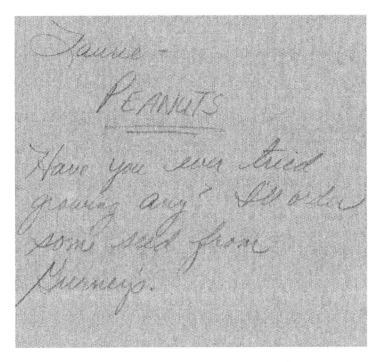

Recipes were another mode of communication for Sue. Depending on the crop coming into season, she would find a favorite recipe and slip it into my box.

Pumpkin Spice Cookies
Bake 375°
for 15 min.

1/2 cup shortening
1 cup brown sugar
2 eggs
1 cup pumpkin puree
2 cups flour
1 T baking powder
2 t cinnamon
1/4 t salt, nutmeg, allspice

Cream tog. shortening + sugar, beat in eggs, blend in puree, add dry ingred. drop by rounded teaspoonfuls onto lightly greased baking sheets

Described as a "traditional teacher," Sue's metamorphosis was occurring in the garden. Two of her closest colleagues smiled with pride as they described the night that she came back to school and sprayed a herbicide to kill the grass across the side of the school building to make way for a new flower bed. "This is a new Sue!" We all reveled in her newly found independence and blatant disregard for the district bureaucracy governing the school grounds. Sue's inspiration for expansion of the garden didn't end with this flower bed. She has since approached me with specifications for a raised herb bed, native wildflower garden, and, perhaps her most grandiose idea, an orchard. What is most impressive about Sue's transformation is her ability not only to voice her creative ideas but also to put them into action. Sue was the teacher who was the first to apply for a grant to support the garden endeavor. She used the grant dollars to purchase garden tools and supplies for the entire school. Like a painter's brushes and oils, these tools represented the implements necessary for her creative expression. Sue was an innovator in the use of the garden for personalized and localized teaching and learning. Before my arrival, she had designed her own cross-curricular lesson centered on the design and selection of perennials for their new flower bed.

My role was becoming more clearly defined. I was there to listen and nurture these women's voices, encouraging their creative acts of meaning.

we enjoyed the creativity.

Sue's creative expressions opened my eyes to a new way of understanding the garden at Jonesville School. I was thinking about the garden no longer as a way to improve student academic performance on an assessment-driven curriculum. Rather, I saw the garden as a way of satisfying teachers' and children's contained urge to create. Betty, after twenty-five years of teaching, had a renewed interest in her practice because of the potential for self-expression that she found in the garden.

> *Fieldnote (8 May 2000): It was really inspiring to see all that Betty had done. She had bought pot makers (seedling starters made out of newspaper) with her own money, created garden journals for the children, developed garden math lessons, procured compost and soil, and made stepping-stones for the garden as an art project.*

Perhaps the most important lesson I learned from Betty was to honor and respect local knowledge and creativity. Without ever saying a word, Betty helped me see that the Jonesville School teachers did not want or need yet another curriculum developed by experts from a thousand miles away. She was the first to gently steer me away from my imported curriculum and to work with me to develop appropriate lessons locally. Betty accomplished this by sharing with me a book called *Native American Gardening*; you see, she wanted to follow her Native American ancestry and plant a "three sisters" *milpa*. This was a transformative moment for us both; I let go of the prefabricated garden curriculum and she let go of the district pacing guide. Together we entered the freedom of letting go, guided by the wisdom of her ancestors.

Following the tradition of Wampanoag gardens, we planted corn, beans, squash, and sunflowers. Beans were planted encircling the mounds of corn according to the four points on the compass. The corn and bean mounds were then interplanted with squash to shade the ground. We planted giant sunflowers as a border to our three sisters garden. I will never forget the delight expressed on the children's faces upon returning to school in August, finding the beans had in fact used the corn stalks as a trellis. The stalks were laden with ears of ripening golden corn, all surrounded by fifteen-foot tall sunflowers. Betty's creative endeavor was richly rewarding for all of us. We were nourished, mind, body, and spirit.

Creativity was sprouting in other areas of the garden. Affirmed by the success of the giant turnip emergent lesson, Carol and Gloria continued to look to the garden for inspiration in their planning. These confident

and experienced teachers saw the dynamics of a living garden as a perfect match for their philosophy of teaching and learning. Explaining that real learning is difficult to plan, Gloria said to me, "We often 'plan' after the fact, or 'plan' as we go." Chuckling, Carol added, "Gloria and I call this planning in the doorway." Planning in the doorway. And isn't this the nature of all learning and inquiry? I saw this in my own feeble attempts to plan or propose this research project: I was now letting go of my plans and developing my own situated methodology or "plan in the doorway."

My collaboration with Gloria and Carol has been one of the most rewarding experiences of this project. The creative lessons we have generated together throughout the year have grown into an entire immersion literacy process, lovingly referred to as "Books We Have Eaten." Attempting to describe how this process evolved, Gloria mused, "Food emerged in the garden, we found a book, designed a lesson, ate it, and then hooked it to the curriculum." Nature drove the process, not the curriculum guide; we had turned the system on its head. This was key. One of my favorite examples of this emergent epistemology evolved around our gigantic pumpkin.

During my first few weeks at Jonesville School, the students in Carol and Gloria's classes decided that they would like to grow pumpkins as a representative of orange in their ROYGBIV (red, orange, yellow, green, blue, indigo, violet) rainbow garden. Little did we know at the time that our orange pumpkins would explode into much more than a rainbow. After the frost-free date for our region, we planted two tiny pumpkin plants in our rainbow garden. Typical of these plants in our cool climate, they hadn't grown much by the time the children left for summer vacation. Pumpkins had not made much of an impression by June 15. However, upon the students' return in August, everything had changed. Something pretty darn close to magic had occurred during those warm days of summer: a very large pumpkin had taken the place of scrawny plants and a monster now sprawled among the corn stalks and tomato vines. Within days, a painted sign was lovingly staked beside it, announcing, "The Biggest Pumpkin Ever." This pumpkin was no ordinary pumpkin; you see, it was going to be the biggest pumpkin ever. And for most of these children, I have no doubt that this was true. For Carol and Gloria, this was the literacy hook they were looking for to make writing come alive. Over the next two months, the teachers used this emergent, living phenomenon to teach the process of writing, culminating in the publication of their very own book entitled, *The Biggest Pumpkin Ever*.

Their creative use of the pumpkin for teaching and learning didn't end there. With the threat of freezing temperatures, the pumpkin had to be harvested and brought inside. Once again, this experiential activity was the perfect teachable moment for Carol and Gloria: "With the garden we can connect backward to the curriculum, we can make up the 'how'." Planning in the doorway one chilly October day, Carol and Gloria decided the pumpkin could be "connected backward" to the estimation and weight curriculum. Wanting the entire class of forty to experience the weight of the pumpkin, we had the children carry in the pumpkin on a bedsheet. Each child was able to participate by holding onto a tiny fistful of sheet. This tiny fistful, however, was a very important step in community building for these children: one pumpkin could be shared by forty, simultaneously. Once inside, we rounded up a couple of old bathroom scales and the next lesson emerged organically. What did the pumpkin weigh? What is a reasonable guess? How much do you weigh? How much does an adult weigh? Do you think you weigh as much as the pumpkin? How can we find out? Post-It notes went around the room, estimations were made, and the final weigh-in revealed that we had grown the biggest (fifty-three-pound) pumpkin ever at Jonesville School.

Halloween came and went without any move to turn our pumpkin into a jack-o'-lantern. With the flurry of activity surrounding the months of November and December, the biggest pumpkin ever took a backseat to other more pressing demands. We turned our calendars to a new year and still there at the front of this busy classroom, shrouded in its ceremonial harvest sheet, was the biggest pumpkin ever. Here is where the story turns quite wondrous.

> *Fieldnote (22 Feb 2001): What a great day. Who would have ever thought you could still be using the garden in the middle of winter! Carol called yesterday and said the children were demanding that we do something with the pumpkin, so we decided to cut it open today. The pumpkin was as fresh and crisp as any pumpkin harvested in October. We all were amazed. We used it to learn counting by tens and grouping hundreds. It was the perfect lesson. We had 563 seeds.*

The emergent creativity did not end with pumpkin-seed math; it was then collectively decided that we would design our very own seed packets and sell the remaining seeds for a tidy profit.

This learning activity emerged naturally, whereas advanced planning would have changed the dynamics, ignoring the interest and curiosity of the teachers and students. Gloria commented to me, "Giving us a cur-

riculum makes it a requirement. We enjoyed the creativity of asking, 'How can growing pumpkins be a literacy activity?'" Carol echoed the same sentiments: "It is so new; we feel privileged to be in on the *molding* of this curriculum." By staying open to the unfolding process, we had tapped into the powerful creative forces with authentic learning. Relinquishing control and heightening my sensitivity to the pressing daily needs of the teachers, I have come closer to what is "really real" than any research objectives could ever anticipate.

> *Fieldnote (3 Feb 2001): This whole "Books We Have Eaten" project we've been working on has blossomed into such a collegial endeavor for us. We worked for three hours tonight after school, and we all agreed we haven't laughed this hard in a long time. We ate dinner together and worked right through dinner because we were having so much fun. We joked that the lessons were so good we should sell them and get rich, though we all knew that the friendship that has grown out of this experience was priceless.*

Creative expressions sprang up in numerous classes as a result of this thirty-by-thirty-foot plot of fertile earth. Other teachers were inspired by Carol and Gloria to break out of their heavily mandated days. Toni and Rose also expressed interest in cooking with their students. When I sug-

gested we could make salsa or chili, two successful activities with Carol and Gloria's group, Toni quickly replied, "I want to cook something different, something that the others haven't done yet." This comment underscores the teachers' repressed needs not only to be creative but also to express themselves as *individuals.* Rampant standardization in public schooling has left teachers starved for any sense of individuality. That day I learned that local knowledge was not limited to the boundaries of the school building; we could fine-tune our contexts for learning with even more precision.

Toni and Rose decided they would like to have their students experience homemade pasta sauce—fresh tomatoes, garlic, basil, and olive oil—a simple recipe. I'll never forget one of the naysayers in the building grumbling, "If it isn't Ragu, they won't eat it." After four years, I can state without exception that I have yet to find a child who won't eat something they have grown. When children are connected to the sacred act of growing food to nourish themselves, they always participate in the ritual with gusto. If they grew it and cooked it, they'll eat it. Further, their bodies were starved for nutritious food. It was not simply a matter of taste with these children; it was a matter of hunger. And so the third graders harvested a basket of red-ripe tomatoes on that warm September afternoon, and we filled the hallways with the aroma of simmering tomatoes and garlic. The kids emulated Emeril, the celebrity chef, by shouting "bam!" as they tossed in fresh oregano to the sauce. Pasta sauce not from a jar, but rather, from the mingling of tiny hands with Mother Earth.

this has gone cross-curricular.

Stephen Toulmin (1982) reminds us to view disciplinary boundaries as historical "accidents." Witnessing the strain against these accidental boundaries in my work with the teachers and students of Jonesville School, I have come to believe that the garden is an escape from the confines of disciplinarity. Corn seeds, ladybugs, children, and pumpkins know nothing of these artificial confines. Elementary schoolteachers feel closer akin to a way of knowing that cannot be subdivided into tidy categories. During a conversation I had with Carol, she explained her frustrations with the current mandated curriculum: "We work with isolated content that is handed down and treated like secondary-content areas. We need a holistic elementary model." Kristan echoed this concern: "There has been no communication between the writers of our state curriculum in the four core areas, none. I want to find the social science connection [in the garden], not just the science." Carol chimed in, "The garden helps us draw connections across the curriculum—it's the scaffolding." The natural linkages are actually impossible to avoid when working at the intersection of plants and people.

Perhaps my favorite example of these cross-curricular linkages created in the garden came from our "biggest pumpkin ever." This one pumpkin generated lessons in literacy (the children wrote a book about the life of this pumpkin), mathematics (the children guessed the weight, estimated the number of pumpkin seeds, counted the seeds in base ten), social studies (an entire economics unit was developed around the creation of pumpkin-seed packets to sell at their spring market), and of course science (the water cycle, life cycle of plants, weather, food webs, and so on). All from one pumpkin.

At the lower-elementary-school level, the teachers had found a rich body of children's literature to reinforce these connections, often with a moral of humanitarian values or caring. Our favorites include *Thundercakes*, *The Carrot Seed*, *Stone Soup*, and *The Gigantic Turnip*. Carol wisely summarized the importance of literature in support of the garden this way: "A story connection as opposed to a scientific connection is much better at this age." I wonder if perhaps it isn't better at any age.

CHAPTER THREE

A place for connection.

A culture of separation will collapse of its own incoherence.
We need communities of memory that experience time
as a continuous flow, a shared rhythm.

—Robert Bellah, *Habits of the Heart*

The data speak clearly to the garden as a place for connection: connection to one another, to food, to place, to ritual, and to me. I witnessed the common unity—the community—that occurs when people work side by side toward a shared vision. But to say that shared vision and a little bit of leadership is all that is needed misses the deeper message of the garden. The garden became a place of connection because it operated according to different rhythms from schooling. You cannot hurry a garden; it is beholden to a temporal pace, unaffected by human clocks and schedules. Stepping out of the classroom and into the garden, one entered a place of slow rhythmic continuity. For our students, the garden offered an alternative to the discontinuity and fragmentation of our modern culture. Questions of personal gain versus collective good seemed to slip away in our garden ecosystem.

Fieldnote (9 Sep 2000): Full, full day. The Hmong girls worked with me today in the garden. These little ones so identify with the

garden. It requires no explanation from me. They immediately grabbed hoes, rakes, and trowels and took to the earth. It appears to be a very communal act for them. They stick together and chatter in their native tongue while they work the soil.

Being together with friends tending the garden was by no means limited to a specific ethnic group. The student garden journals were full of entries that reflect the communal nature of gardening:

Garden thought- I like the garden because me, Andrew, Charlie, and brad got to rake the garden and plant corn it was really fun.

I like the garden because me and Jarret raked it.

. . . and I get to Be with my Friend and I Love to be outside and my Friend is with me.

. . . the most thing I liked was Being outside with Alice Grines.

I liked helping the youngers.

Released from the culture of separation and individual gain that is transmitted in schooling, the Jonesville students reveled in the freedom to work together for communal good.

> *Fieldnote (5 Sep 2000): Today during lunch, I was hoeing by myself just to get on top of the weeds, and as soon as the kids were let outside for recess, three girls came and asked if they could help me. I told them to go get more hoes, and sure enough they came back with hoes and joined me. Amazing, hoeing weeds instead of recess!*

One morning while tilling our "Little Red Hen Wheat Field," I experienced this pull of the earth once again. Several classes were released for morning break, and before I knew it the kids had formed a conga line (hands to waist, hands to waist) behind me to share in this ritual tilling of the earth. Up and down the rows we marched behind the tiller, mysteriously drawn together by the freshly plowed earth.

Ultimately, I found that this sense of connection crossed grade levels and generations. Parents, teachers, brothers, sisters, and grandparents were mentioned in connection with the garden. Frequently, children from upper grade levels asked if they could help work with the younger children in the garden, anything from explaining the benefits of worms to distinguishing weeds from tender seedlings. Radiating ever outward, the garden helped sustain fragile familial connections:

> "Nicole my best friend gave me some sunflower seeds and I took them home and my dad cooked them. He put them in this circle thing on the stove and put salt on them and we ate 'em. My sister wanted some more but there wasn't no more."

> "I took a tomato home and shared it with my sister and brother, and we put salt on it and it tasted good."

> "Mrs. Thorp, when we have the popcorn party can I bring my Grandma?"

Teachers often connected to one another in the garden during breaks and recess to monitor the progress of the vegetables or to discuss pathways (always an issue with so many feet), labels, mulching, the challenges of composting, or recipes for whatever crop was in season. Food is a universal connector. Alice, a fifth-grade teacher, observed that the schoolwide enthusiasm generated by the garden reminded her of "the feeling experienced long ago when communities would celebrate the harvest together." Proudly standing among the beans and corn of our three sisters garden, Betty concurred: "I see the garden as a way to develop self-sufficiency, to learn that survival depends on everybody." I have no doubt that the children at Jonesville School have come a long way in learning this lesson. Tending the earth together with the women and children of Jonesville, one begins to understand the Greek concept of cosmos: to share once again in a common "good order" of the universe.

During a photo elicitation session one afternoon with several second graders, I heard repeatedly the importance of being with others while gardening, cooking, and eating. It seemed that these children understood intuitively the importance of these connections even though our fast-food culture has stripped this from their lives. Vying for my attention, three of my garden buddies chattered away, "I love you, garden [note the personal pronoun] and tomatoes and sunflowers and Mrs. Thorp and wheat and cucumber and corn and pumpkins and squash and most of all Mrs. Thorp and Mrs. Price." Tugging at my shirt, another child interrupted, "I have one more sentence: We made the salsa from the garden and had a salsa party." Finally the voices subsided and one last concern was voiced, "Does Mrs. Lander have a garden spot?" The point I wish to make here is that it is not just the fresh garden produce, or the cooking, or the eating. It is the entire communal ritual. The children are telling us something, and we need to listen: fast food is destroying the very fabric of our society. Thomas Jefferson preached this, and our children are repeating the very same message. Our connection to the land will make us who we are as a people.

connecting to rituals of food.

I came to this study to connect children to the healing rhythms of a garden, and soon discovered that the garden served a far more basic need—filling empty stomachs. Many of the children in this study came to school hungry. "Do you know what hunger smells like?" a teacher asked me with a penetrating gaze. "I do. I smell it on their breath every day. How can I teach when I know they are hungry?" Her colleague chimed in, "Yup, that's why afternoon kindergarten didn't work. Remember? They all showed up hungry. Impossible." Historically, women have always participated in the cultivation of food; it is only since the industrialization of modern agriculture that we have become so dissociated with the intimate act of feeding our loved ones with the fruits of the earth. And so cooking our homegrown produce became an integral part of the garden experience, emerging directly from our feminine instinct to nourish these children of poverty. To focus solely on scientific experimentation in our garden would have grossly missed the point—remaining hostage to the intellectual culture of science while ignoring the larger issues of existence. Recipes began appearing in my mailbox, and the most common question became "Laurie, when can we cook again?"

Gustavo Esteva (1994) speaks of the fire at the heart of communal life, a primal organizing principle called *comida*. Difficult to translate, *comida* refers to a sense of community where scarcity cannot appear. *Comida* as I understand it is much more than cooking food: it is a complex cultural relationship that exists at the intersection of woman, fire, and the fruits of the earth. It is an ethic of caring that we have nearly lost with modernity. I have no doubt that *comida* is what we were experiencing.

> *Fieldnote (19 Dec 2000): Second grader Vanessa asked me for a hug today and wouldn't let go. I told her I loved her, and then she looked me deep in the eyes and asked, "When are we gonna cook again?" Translation—when are we going to go to that safe space of* comida, *that space where there is no threat of scarcity.*

Our food rituals had the ability to unite us across time, politics, generations, gender, social class, and culture. The day after our salsa party, little James, thirty years my junior, put his arm around me, motioning me to lean down for a private conversation, and whispered, "I thought you was gonna save me some more of that salsa." Gloria, while brainstorming with her students about what to do with their bumper crop of tomatoes, recollected Sunday evenings as a child, cooking homemade tomato soup with her father. Andrea, a recent immigrant from Haiti, stubbornly refused to leave the kitchen each time we cooked; much like music, cooking requires no translation—she was at home again—chopping and dicing were her mother tongue. Gordon, our school custodian, saw me lugging a pumpkin to the kitchen and asked if we wouldn't like to try his recipe for pumpkin coffee cake. Following one of our many salsa sessions, teachers from nearly every grade wandered in to sample and unwind after a long day of teaching. The unplanned warmth and collegiality that occurred around a simple bowl of salsa provided as much for the teachers that day as it did for the students.

For the children of Jonesville School, gardening had become intimately intertwined with cooking and eating, which was reason to garden again next year. Perhaps this was their first small step toward constructing a cosmology of interdependence rather than dominance. They had witnessed that by caring for their tiny patch of earth, Mother Earth reciprocated with great bounty. Pondering a photograph of the garden one cold winter day, Timmy thought long and hard then looked straight into my eyes, "I remember the popcorn; we didn't eat it yet. I can hardly wait to eat it." Matthew Fox (1995) says we need a "revolution in ritual." He reminds us that ritual is how cultures pass on their values to the young. I am encouraged by all of our food rituals this year: planting winter wheat shoulder to shoulder in a circle, harvesting the great pumpkin, shucking popcorn knee to knee on the floor to mention just a few. I can't help but believe that we have transmitted the value of food as a celebration of life. We have participated in the sacred ritual of food with our hands, feet, nose, heart, and mind.

connecting to the gifts of place.

One afternoon while working on "Books We Have Eaten," I had the opportunity to talk with Carol and Gloria about a notion of place that I had found in the literature and experienced in my own life. I wondered aloud if it would be possible for these children to develop a sense of place here at school through the garden. Carol began by saying, "I have become more and more aware that the children have a very fuzzy concept of how the land is connected to them. Place is absent from their lives. At Pine and Maple Streets there is this massive trailer park; these kids have street skills that mirror our inner-city kids. The vast majority is not allowed to go outside, let alone connect and develop a sense of place." Gloria chimed in, "I want to make that stewardship connection, but I'm tired of the environmental preaching; generation upon generation have missed this opportunity." We agreed that the garden was an alternative to pedantic preaching. The conversation then turned to memories from our childhood "places" and the lasting connections to the earth that we made. However, the gifts of our summer childhood places by the lake and in the forest are only a dream for these children. Largely, these children were dis-placed people, through no fault of their own, never able to truly inhabit a place. They did not have access to nature, nor were they given the freedom and time to "soak in a place" as Paul Shepard (1977) says is so necessary for healthy human development.

However tentative, our little garden has provided the teachers and the children of Jonesville School with many gifts of place.

First, is the gift of peace.

Fieldnote (19 Sep 2000): Arrived early to Toni's room, walked in while she was talking to the kids about her experience with the garden. She was telling them that she would come out to the garden in the summer and it was like therapy. She said, "I'd be all alone and the only thing around was the deer. It was so peaceful."

I had the privilege of witnessing this "therapy" of peace with another teacher one day while weeding. Quite unexpectedly, late one afternoon, Millie, a classroom aide, appeared in the garden and began pulling weeds. The image was incongruous because she had on a dress and good shoes on this warm June day. Very soon it became apparent to me that she needed this space to work through some personal angst in her life. No matter the mud on her shoes or the pulling of weeds in a dress, of greater import was being surrounded by the soothing rhythms of the garden. Betty had once described these rhythms as "a sense of order" amid chaos. Millie pulled the weeds in silence for quite a while, making order in her mind; or perhaps, it was just a quieting of the mind that accompanies good, hard physical labor. Whatever the precise therapeutic effect had been, Millie soon was able to articulate her angst verbally and, within an hour or so, leave in a different state of mind.

The calming effect of the garden was not limited only to teachers; children responded, too. Eric, a particularly challenging student, was being detained in the classroom for not having completed his work. Defiantly, he stated to his teacher that he didn't want to plant anything in the garden. Finally, work completed, Eric was allowed to come with me into the garden. Eric picked up a hand trowel and angrily stabbed the soil. "Kill, kill, kill," he chanted. Trusting the transformative powers of Mother Earth, I let Eric work out his anger at the world. After about an hour of angrily engaging with the garden project, he slowly dropped his cool, hard facade and admitted, "This garden is going to be cool." Other compelling testimonials to the therapeutic effect of the garden were found in the students' journals:

We enjoy it. Its soothing listening to the bees, clipping weeds, and getting good results.

Gardens make me feel relaxed because the smell of the vegetibles and flowers.

These entries were especially revealing; for me they conveyed that our garden was a haven of calm for two often overlooked reasons: it didn't *sound* like a school, and it didn't *smell* like a school.

The second gift was the gift of joy. From my very first day on this project, I noticed that children connect to the earth without any necessary instruction. They were drawn to the fallow soil like a magnet. I couldn't keep them away. The minute I would show up at the school, children would glom on to my every available appendage, dragging me out into the garden. "What are we going to do today?" "Can I help?" "Will you tell Mrs. Brown I'm out here with you?" It was so damn easy.

"I like the garden
'cause I get to go outside."
Me too little one,
me too.
Very soon,
you will live a life
mostly indoors.
Stuffy,
Windowless,
Nine to five.
Take my hand,
let's go explore.
You say you think
"the garden is just the right size."
Hold on to your contentment
little one.
So few of us ever arrive there.
Yes,
it is
just the right size.
Enough.
This priceless moment is enough.
May it last you a lifetime.

The garden journals were full of entries that expressed the children's delight in their garden experiences:

9/14/00
Tom

Tom — Last year there was not
even plantes this year
there are lots of planters.
ther are pumpkins tomatose
and sun flowers and ther
are butifl

One of the most grateful recipients of this gift from the garden was our school custodian. An unexpected consequence of this project, I was thrilled to discover this connection.

Fieldnote (11 Jul 2000): We proceeded to the back garden and found everything growing really well. No pests and no diseases. The custodian (Joan) came out and said, "I could just spend my whole day out here going from one garden plot to the next, weeding, watering, and eating."

The third gift of place was the gift of beauty. The students and teachers of Jonesville School recognized and appreciated this newly found beauty but also expressed interest in protecting and expanding the beauty of their surroundings. The importance of beauty and beautiful surroundings was underscored as a core value at Jonesville School during a conversation I had with Dee, the principal. Exuding energy and enthusiasm, Dee quickly steered me out of her office to show me her "vision" for the school. She first pointed to the school parking lot and told me that she would like to transform this area with islands of green space and trees. Pointing out from another window she said, "See that strip under those windows, maybe a rock garden or herbs there. I want that whole area to

be a garden. I want children to be hit with the beauty *before* they enter the school." She then took me down the east hallway and pointed to the various windows in the classrooms that at the time looked out on overgrown shrubs. She suggested that we promote an "adopt a window" program to beautify this side of the school. Dee added, "I would love our school to be a place where you are surrounded by beauty." The children from all grade levels concurred:

> "I like to see our school yard look pretty with a garden."
> "We garden because we want to make the school beautiful."
> "I just love the garden because it is just lovely."
> "Next year I'll like more flowers."
> "I think the garden makes our school look nice."

These appreciative expressions for the beauty in the garden were a hopeful sign that tenuous connections were developing. I am convinced that it is difficult to appreciate beauty when you have no sense of connection to place, when you are a displaced person. This is the risk we run as our schools become homogeneous institutions of mandated standardization. We will lose the unique natural beauty that has always been one of our best teachers. Worse yet, we will tacitly transmit the message that learning is an ugly, indoor, predictable affair and that beauty is somehow peripheral to education, reserved only for the privileged. What a mistake this would be.

connection to the garden lady.

I came to Jonesville School to help children connect to the earth and found in the process that we became connected to one another. The importance of this message is not what I personally brought to the project, but rather what it speaks to: the urgent needs of our children and the impossible demands placed before our teachers. My regular presence in the garden created a venue where children and teachers could experience a living, reciprocal cosmos quite different from the fragmented, time-crunched experience of mandated schooling.

Fieldnote (19 Dec 2000): Today in the hallway, a little guy stopped me and asked if the wheat was going to be okay. Yes, yes, winter wheat will do just fine under a blanket of snow, just wait, you'll see.

As these connections stabilized and grew, I noticed the important role I played as mediator in these new relationships. While working with the children, they often would seek reassurance from me: "Mrs. Thorp, do you know it rained last night?" "Laurie, are these ready to pick?" "Will our sweet peas survive?" Underscoring this at lunch one day, Carol said, "You know, it's not *just* the garden; it's you."

> *Fieldnote (9 Sep 2000): Went to Alice's room at 2:30 p.m. to make salsa. Alice was so appreciative that I would do this with her class. She said, "This is so awesome that you'd come in and do this with the kids." I replied that I was grateful she would give me the time in her busy day. She replied, "Are you kidding, nobody is willing to come in and do this with them, to let them cook. I don't even think their parents take the time to do this."*

Time. The garden beckons to organize our lives not according to clock time—*chronos*—but rather to *kairos*—sacred time. I am convinced this is one of the most important consequences of school gardening with "The Garden Lady." We had time on our side. During one of my many insightful conversations with Carol and Gloria, Carol reflected on our experience together, "Elementary teachers are expected to be jack-of-all-trades, master of none. Then a master comes in, and it allows for that moment: time for us to become masters. Laurie made that happen." Together with the rhythms of the garden, I made space for "that moment" that we all long for. Tragically, our students are starved for these "moments" with a patient elder. This is how wisdom is passed down through the generations. It seems that we are obsessed with moving ahead as fast as we can with very little concern for the wisdom of our elders. Carol described this as her "Andy Griffith theory of learning." Her theory goes something like this: when teaching a difficult or new concept "get folksy, do the Andy and Opie thing," take it slow and tell a personal story. "Kids remember this, they remember my reminiscent stories or the Garden Lady talking about the land." Armed with this powerful image of Andy and Opie, I embraced the "Andy Griffith theory of learning" and became the "folksy" patient elder with an expanse of time and blue sky as my classroom.

"Kids remember this . . . " and remember, they did. Sitting crouched on pint-size chairs, facilitating photo elicitation with a second-grade garden buddy, I queried, "Is there anything else you want to tell me about the garden?" A tiny person looked me in the eyes and earnestly replied, "That you helped us plant the garden." The food, cooking, and friends were all mentioned as important components, but someone older and wiser made the circle of learning complete.

One of the joys of working with this heart-wide-open age group was their unabashed ability to connect so deeply in a matter of weeks. I started to notice these connections forming very early on when I was sitting in the "teaching chair" (in itself an extension of trust), charting the children's ideas for their rainbow garden. While we talked, I noticed little fingers inching toward my clogs, trying to touch me. Very soon, these tenuous connections expanded to clutching my pant leg and warm and sweaty hand-holding.

> *Fieldnote (1 Oct 2000): While outside, Timmy thought I was walking away to leave, so he quickly grabbed my hand and said, "Where are you going? Can I come with you?" I reassured him that I wasn't leaving. He now calls me "My Laurie" when his classmates are around.*

I may be *his* Laurie but to fellow classmate Vanessa, I am "Mommy." I am not sure what triggered Vanessa's color-blind (for she is African American) identification with me, but I suspect it has to do with the holy trinity of woman, fire, and food.

> "I come down to the water to cool my eyes, but everywhere I look I see fire; that which isn't flint is tinder, and the whole world sparks and flames."
> —Annie Dillard, *Pilgrim at Tinker Creek*

CHAPTER

FOUR

Wonder.

"Wonder is my second favorite condition to be in, after love . . . "
—David James Duncan, "Four Henry Stories"

I f there is any hope for reinvigorating our system of science education, I believe it will be found not by increased teacher accountability, not with more rigorous scientific curricula, but rather through our sense of wonder. I am guilty, I'll admit; I arrived on the scene thinking that by connecting garden activities to the state-mandated science curriculum, I could somehow save the day. Instead, what I found was, at the heart of scientific inquiry is good, old-fashioned, slack-jawed wonder. "Mrs. Thorp, look at how big this turnip is!" "Laurie, the wheat is up!" In our push to quantify academic achievement, we have got it all backward. As Eliot Eisner (2002) suggests, the kind of schools we need should be as interested in the questions children pose to the world as in the answers they give. Our schools have become obsessed with a single set of correct answers when in fact the most intellectually challenging task is not in finding correct answers but rather in posing questions. However, it is difficult to pose questions to a world you know nothing about. The garden animated the world for these children. Over and over, I heard teachers tell me that these children had very limited life experiences. When you're an inner-city, latchkey kid, told to stay indoors, a thirty-by-thirty-foot garden is a big wide world of wonder:

. . . last year I platted a pumkin and it was a seed then. When we lefed last year I thoght it whont grow intill aroud my birthday. But I guees not it is big.

When we came back from summer the sunfowers wer hege the punkins wer hege to . . .

I want to tell you about the stem on the sunflower when I took the sunflower top off I found a little caterpillar and took him and put him by the tomatoes.

We grew sunflowers and corn almost as tall as our school!

There was more than just one pumpkin on the vine in our rainbow garden there were three!

Rupert Sheldrake (Sheldrake and Fox 1996) asks scientific colleagues why they do what they do and in almost every case the answers trace back to some primal moment of wonder. Perhaps for one or two of these children, these moments of wonder would place them on a trajectory of inquiry and exploration that otherwise they may have never known.

> *Fieldnotes (16 Oct 2000): The sunflower seeds are magical for the kids. When we returned to the classroom, Jason came to me with one sunflower seed in his hand. Pressing through the clamoring and clinging of his classmates, I could tell he needed to ask me something very important. First he asked me if he could have it, "Of course Jason, of course." Then he wanted to know what would happen if he planted it at home, "If I water it every day, will it grow? Will it get a big stalk too? How deep do I plant it?"*

I know that glorious autumn day Jason felt the gravitational forces of wonder pulling him in a new direction. That a seed no bigger than your thumbnail could be transformed into a fifteen-foot green canopy was pure wonder. And to see wonder through a child's eyes as I did that day was to fall in love with the world all over again.

they are so removed from experience.

For the children of Jonesville School, the garden provided a complex, living environment, ripe for experiential learning. The teachers often stressed the importance of the garden as a space for children to expand their life experiences, a place to interact with nature increasingly absent in their lives. We found the flora and fauna of our garden provided the much-needed scaffolding teachers were always searching for. However, it was the words of a third grader that spoke most directly to this point. Following a garden planning session with Toni's class, I asked the children if there were any questions; fielding questions about planting space, and vegetable varieties,

I was stunned when a brave little girl queried, "What is it like to garden?" So alien to my childhood experience, this question was in essence asking me: What is it like to breathe? How could I explain something so tied up with who I am. This tiny little question, this baffling Zen koan, went straight for the heart and left me floundering for words. If I could wave your words on a banner for all to see, little one, I would. Frantically signaling an SOS like a semaphore, lost at sea, I want the world to hear you. I struggle to get this right. With this awesome responsibility, I will pound out your tender question in the wee hours of this night knowing I will never rest until the ground thaws, and I can take your hand in mine, to show you what it is to garden.

Contrasted against the concrete and asphalt terrain of their neighborhoods, the rich textures of a living garden were a feast for the senses. Once again, the local wisdom of the children reminded me that the simple sensations of the garden should not be overlooked in an academic quest for highbrow findings constructed to wow school boards and educational experts.

"I like to go in the garden 'cause there was a lot of stuff to look at."

" . . . or just to smell the fowers it [was a] refreshing smell."

"My favorite is the sunflowers and the big pumpkin because I like the colors."

"I went to the garden today and got to touch the plants like butternut scotch."

"We got to walk through the garden was fun. When I was waiting, a bee chased me and I ran away."

"My favorite place in the garden was the sunflowers 'cause the sunflowers are hanging down and it was like a jungle."

"I like the bachelor buttons because they are blue!"

"It was fun picking the popcorn, and it was fun growing it, and looking at it and peeling it."

Like sailors returning from months at sea, increasingly our children come to us in a state of sensory deprivation. Strip malls and urban blight is what greets our children today. I think we can do better. These homesick mariners deserve a parade of song sparrows and chickadees, tadpoles and tree frogs, hollyhocks and pole beans. The school-yard garden is my attempt at this hero's welcome—welcome to planet Earth.

one thing i like is turning up soil.

For many, being in the garden meant a chance to dig in the soil. I was surprised at the importance of this simple act of "turning up soil." The students of Jonesville School weren't concerned about getting their hands dirty; in fact they reveled in it. Hands first, they plunged into the soil looking for rocks and worms or simply digging.

Fieldnote (9 May 2000): Jason really took to the garden today. We were raking out all the stones and preparing an area for planting. He took great delight in digging up worms and bringing them to show me. He would then take his handful of worms to his personal squash mound. A little girl from Julie's class wandered into the

garden while we were working. She was new to this school and to this country—a recent Somali immigrant, drawn to the soil like a magnet, you could tell by her expression that in these unfamiliar surroundings, the garden somehow felt familiar. Without words, she immediately took a hoe and began digging in the earth.

Working the soil is an international language that crosses all boundaries of race, ethnicity, and class. It is also a seminal springtime ritual. After our long midwestern winters, we celebrate the season by plunging our hands into the soil. Children are no exception; they yearn for this opportunity to reconnect with the earth.

Which leads me to one of the most delightful experiences of my time at Jonesville School. Not one week into the project, I was working with a group of fourth graders, preparing their section of the garden for planting. It was a glorious day in May, and I had been entrusted with ten rambunctious students wielding rakes, hoes, and shovels. Walking out to the garden I thought to myself, my God, what have I gotten myself into? They could kill one another with these tools. Not to worry, the children were so thrilled to be out of doors on this fine day, they took right to the soil like seasoned farmers. The warmth of the sun and the loose, rich soil began to work their magic on us all. For Rodney, it was just too much to bear; before I could respond, he had slung off his shoes and socks and slowly walked the entire length of the garden, smiling from ear to ear. I tell you, it is primal. We are hardwired to press our flesh against Mother Earth, and when we are deprived of this intimacy we are somehow diminished as a people. Had I not been so new to the school that day I would have encouraged all to partake of this wonderful rite of spring. Now three years later, I have become the trusted Garden Lady, and as the soil thaws we dream our barefoot dreams.

can i have one to take home?

I have to tell you that I've saved the best for last. Hold on to your hearts— they don't get any better than this. This is what makes research so damn rewarding. Just when you least expect it, the data jump out at you with a showstopper. And the best part, I can really toot the horn on this one 'cause I didn't figure it out, nope, not me. I puzzled and puzzled, cogitated and scrutinized, and finally yelled uncle. So I took this heap of data to Kristan and cried, "Help." She looked at it briefly, and took my breath away with her powers of insight and interpretation. But I get ahead of

myself here; first let me tell you about what got stuck in my craw and wouldn't let go. Children have a way of doing that, you know.

> *Fieldnote (18 Sep 2000): Shelley has been trying to get my atten-*
> *tion all week to look at her giant sunflower. During the morning*
> *break, she sat peacefully under her sunflower the entire period*
> *gathering seeds. Later in the afternoon, I finally made time to go*
> *with her and look at it—only after she came up to me and dra-*
> *matically emptied out her pockets with the seeds she had harvested.*
> *She was so proud of her stash and the flower that produced it,*
> *so together we went and admired her incredible sunflower. Yes,*
> *indeed Shelly, that is one beautiful sunflower. I asked her what she*
> *would like to do with the seeds, she replied, "Eat some, plant some,*
> *and cook with some."*

That same day, Jason found me and asked if he could collect sunflower seeds, too. But that wasn't enough, he wanted me to stay with him and help. Equally important was the ritual of tasting them together, cracking the shiny-black-seed coats between our teeth and picking out the meaty center. Like Shelley, he wanted to take some home, informing me that he was going to "make a big tray and roast them in the oven with salt." Sunflower seeds were not the only seeds that made their way into the pockets and backpacks of the students. While cleaning up the garden one autumn afternoon, several of the boys rooted through the compost bin to find pumpkin seeds in the cast-off, rotting pumpkins. "Look Laurie! Can we have these?" It was that afternoon that I began to have an inkling that something significant was stirring. What was it about these seeds? Over and over I witnessed the magical connection between children and seeds.

> *Fieldnote (19 Sep 2000): When making salsa today, I saved the seed core from the pepper to show them the seeds. Later while cleaning up, Timmy asked me if he could take it home. I said yes and asked what he was going to do with it, and he replied, "Bury it."*

As if all this seed hoarding wasn't enough to get my attention, the children expressed their desire to take other sacred relics home from the garden. No matter the size, shape, or condition, it was, "Please can I take it home?" Harvesting our bumper crop of cucumbers (we planted an entire packet of cucumber seeds), I was amazed that even the fat, bloated, yellowing cukes lost for months under the tangle of vines found their way into the backpacks. Jason, my little buddy, somehow conned me into three cukes. Those who missed out on the cucumber harvest took to the compost bins to see what treasures they could find. Old zucchini the size of baseball bats were unearthed and gleefully stashed in backpacks.

> *Fieldnote (1 Oct 2000): Second grader Allison begged me for three ears of popcorn today. After several unsuccessful attempts to explain that we didn't have enough for even one ear to go home, I asked her why this was so important to her. She then proceeded to tell me that she needed three because her mom and dad didn't live together and she now lived with her grandmother. What did the corn signify in Allison's broken world?*

Tomatoes were also used as an offering to the fragile family life these children knew so well. During a photo elicitation session, a second grader shared this story with me: "And I want to tell you about the big tomatoes. I brought home a big tomato and my brother and sister wanted to smash it and put salt on it, but I said, 'No! I want to wait until Mom got home to show her and cook it in our spaghetti.' When she got home she said, 'Wow, where did you get that?'"

These stories and experiences kept piling up before me, yet I was unsure what it all meant. Why was it so important to take the fruits of the garden home? Scarcity? Pride? Approval? Was this true of all their school-work? Was there a need to take everything (artwork, science experiments, projects) home? "No," Kristan replied, "the only other time I've seen this was when we worked with clay." With barely a moment's hesitation, and complete certainty in her interpretation, she said, "They are taking seeds and squash home because a teacher never touched it." She continued, rapid-fire, "There has been no interference; you see, tomatoes and cucumbers are safe to go home because they have not been interpreted through the hierarchy of the school. Seeds and gourds are not a school product; they are completely untouched by human hands; they don't bear our stamp of approval." Kristan continued, "Oh yeah, I noticed this. Remember the giant sunflower head you brought in the room, the thirteen pounder? It never exhausted itself. Those kids would pet, pocket, and eat sunflower seeds without ever tiring of the experience. I saw this with the corn seed too. We were using corn in our rainsticks; they couldn't keep their hands out of that tub of corn. There were beads and macaroni to use but they were in no way as powerful as the corn." Kristan and I talked fervently for the next hour about the significance of her interpretation—how education had become so removed from direct experience. In fact, these children are awash in the artifacts of *schooling*. Textbooks, progress reports,

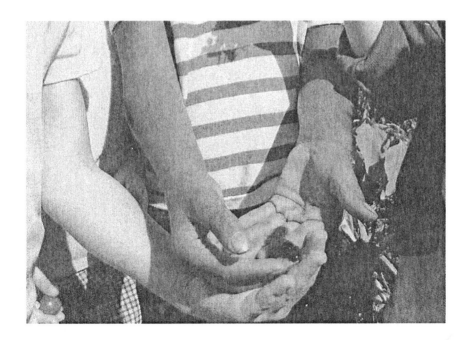

vaccination records, permission slips, all bear the mark of school approval. All are tainted with the scent of authority, slowly stripping away any notion of self-realization. The importance of these school-to-home connections should not be missed. Our bumper crop of cucumbers provided communication home that is welcomed and universally understood. The student-grown vegetables were my message in a bottle sent across the ocean that divides school and home—it reads: look Mom, look at what I accomplished, be proud of me. As our evening drew to a close, Kristan looked me in the eyes and stunned me once again with her powers of perception: "By the way, that is also why the children love you. You're the Garden Lady. They don't associate you with school. Be careful, I've seen it happen before with my volunteers; if you become too closely aligned with the school you'll lose your magic."

Richard Quinney says, "There are many ways to do ethnography, more ways than can be imagined in any philosophy. And amid the ways is the telling of tales beyond any notion of science, objectivity, or rational discourse. Time and death do not wait on the tools of any trade. Imagine wildly the possibilities of ethnography. Perhaps you will make the trip of a lifetime" (1996, 381). Indeed, this has been the trip of a lifetime.

CHAPTER
FIVE

How our garden grows.

The garden looks small when you are not in it,
but when you are in it, it is big.

—Emily, fourth grader

what it looks like.

Jonesville School Elementary has a garden. The garden is in the
back playground. It is by the school's swings and it is where the
school kids and more people can see it. You can get there fast by
walking in the gym and out the door or by the room 115. and you
can get there any way in the school. Miss G's class room is about a
few feet away. Mr. K and the classis are about forthy sakints away
form it. (Allie)

What makes our garden different is the different plants that are
in the garden. Thar are moonfliwrs, corn, sunfliwrs, tumatoew,
papers, qeuwcumbers, putaetos, carets and senses. The garden is

*(This chapter was written entirely by the fourth graders of Jonesville Elementay
School, with a little formatting help from Michael Rodriguez and Nathaniel
Fremuth.)*

like a maze. And it's nature and wonderful. It has so many sounds and tastes. (Brenden)

so many sounds and tastes

so many sounds and tastes

I have no idea what it would be like in a garden but what I do know is that you have to take good care of it unless you want it to die. I saw in Detroit a beautiful garden. (Patrick)

Most people are very excited about there first time to experience a garden like ours. J-ville garden is an amazing piece of nature. My first time in the garden, I was amazed with everything in the garden. My friends and I are working hard to keep our garden

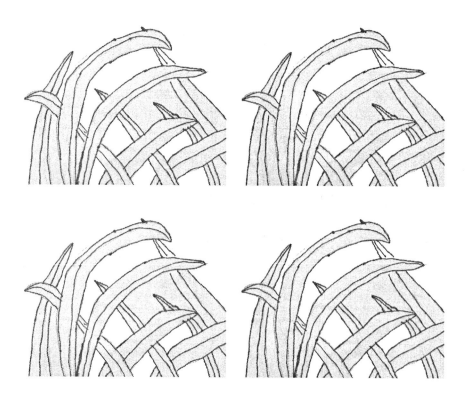

moving on. Each year our garden changes. Ms. Thorp, Mr. Mike, and Mr. Daniel helps us every year to grow plants and foods. (Harley)

You would probably be surprized because most schools don't have gardens. Most people have fun in the garden. How we have fun is find food. Some people are bored in the garden. People are bored because they don't like to garden.

Some kids go in the garden a bunch of times, but some people hate the garden. (Cory)

The two biggest gardens I've ever seen came in a variety of color. When you look at the gardens they're like a radiant blend of sparkling beauty. The gardens smelt like different scented burning candles. In the gardens I've seen, there were carnations, roses, and sunflowers. At Clearwater City, we planted orange blossoms, lilac trees, palm trees, and orange trees. (Trey)

My heart explodes like a good volcano because I get to work in the garden. My reaction is excited when I get to work in the garden because we get to plant delicious food. The fifth grade boys roll in the exsargous [asparagus] and the girls laugh at them. (Allie)

tools we use.

The Tool I Would use is a shovel because I like to dig. I'd dig for planting vegetable and maybe fruit and other things. I can use the hose for watering the plants. (Aurlie)

Every year I use shovels to find different insects and squishy and *slimy* worms. I don't like the slimy worms because there fat and plump. But when your watering with the watering can always be careful that you don't water the plants to much, unless their really dry. We use watering cans to water the flowers, strawberries and many other plants. Every year we plant new plants and every day we water the plants in the spring. Here are some tools you use and need seeds, hose, little and big shovels, sun and small rakes. (Harley)

The kind of tools we used were shovels to dig holes. We used rakes to rake the dirt. You can use your hands for tools to. By cupping them or spreading your fingers you might touch a worm but they wont hurt you. You might see other kinds of bugs to I like regular shovels better then hand shovels. I like hand shovels to because you can see the bugs easier.

By cupping them or spreading your fingers you might touch a *worm* but they wont hurt you.

It is really cool. The kind of bugs you see are worms and spiders are big some spiders are small. (Jacob)

Journal entry

If for some crazy reason you run out of things for a child to do in a garden, you can always, I mean ALWAYS, count on their desire to dig. Today, Daniel and I were working with some kids from Ms. P's class when lunch was released. This happens twice daily; the double doors to the lunchroom burst open, spilling forth newly fueled little

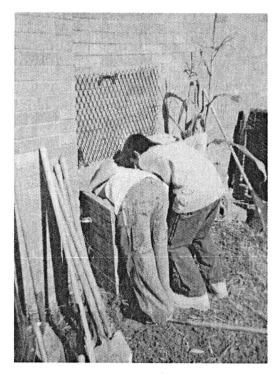

bodies that gravitate to the many steel structures strewn about the grounds behind the school. Naturally, a few of them never make it to the swing set or jungle gym, their attention diverted by the things growing in the garden. And it is at this moment when Jonesville is transformed into a miniature Pamplona, Spain; the living alleyways alive with the movement of stampeding size sixes. Before things get out of hand, Daniel just starts dealing shovels and the holes begin to spread, the chaos is contained . . . at least until the second lunch.

—Mike, university volunteer

In the garden we sometimes have lots fun and we also work and the way we get are work done is by using, tools and the tools we use are shovels rakes and hands and also seeds some times you get dirty using these tool and using these tools is really hard work. (Nathan)

What kinds of tools we need to start a garden are shovels, rakes, hands ✋ to dig with, straw, water so the plants to drink, soil to keep the plants warm. These are all the tools we need. Harvesting is more important because it helps the plants to grow. (Frankie)

I like to dig in the garden. I like raking in the garden. I like to use a hand shovel too. (Andy)

I use tools for digging holes to plant seeds. Sometimes the dirt gets hard so I have to push a little harder to get a hole.

I also see insects when I dig holes the insects I see are worms, ants, and other insects that live underground. The dirt sometimes get dirty and wet also muddy.

Sometimes we use small or big tools to dig holes. Sometimes we kill worms on accident when where digging to plant seeds because we can't see the worm when where digging. We have to take the things out of the garden like food rappers to keep the garden clean. Sometimes people goes to the garden when they see an insect the person thinks the insects gonna hurt the person then they might use one of the tools to kill the insect that is in the persons way. We sometimes use food in the garden to make soup and salsa for us to eat. (Vachee)

I don't now much about the J-Ville garden. I've never been in or had a garden because I just moved here from Alaska. But I now what tools we need. We need shovels, seeds, water, love, sun, sticks and plastic clear tent and gloves . . . I read it in a book. I saw it on Martha Stewart. You can plant a lot of seeds I know what seeds you need you can have sunflower seeds, pumpkin seeds, watermelon seeds and so much more. Those are the things you need to make a garden. I feel very full when I eat all the fruits and vegetables. (Celena)

watering the garden.

In the garden the water is an important part. The water helps the animals and the plants grow better. If plants do not get water plants will dry out and never grow. Sometimes we would use watering cans and use the hose. But what you have to do is make sure that the water is cold. There are a lot of plants that grow in the Jonesville garden. Every one loves the food that we grow. You should make a garden of your own. So that when you want a vegetable you can eat whenever you want. (Ashley)

YOU SHOULD MAKE
A GARDEN OF YOUR OWN!

Before you water anything first, you have to have something to plant, like peas, corn, asparagus, sunflowers, strawberries, and more!

I like watering because it is cold. I also like watering because you can hold a hose. You can feel the coldness through the material that the hose is made out of. The hose is heavy and long. It can be different colors, but the main color is green. (Morgan)

Every spring I know that I am going to start watering the flowers and plants with the hose. I feel *excited* when I start watering the

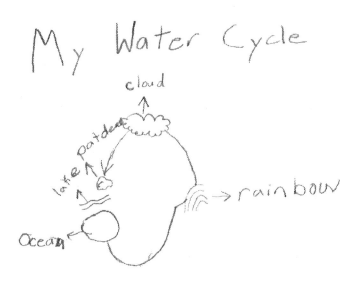

flowers because *I can't wait until the plants and flowers grow.* We water the plants and flowers because if we don't water them they won't grow and they will die. We water lots of thing. (Aurelie)

The water is fun because it's cold when you wash your hands after you have been in the garden, in the soil planting seeds. Water is also helpful to the food in the garden that the Jonesville School has grown. The Jonesville School has fun growing plants and watering them because, Dr. Thorp, Mr. Daniel, Sarah, and Mr. Mike enjoy working with us. The seeds we plant are strawberries, corn, carrots, lettuce, and lots MORE!! (Morgan)

There are a lot of people likes to water the garden. A lot of people likes to water the garden because the person likes to do things in the garden. We have to water a plant that is dry. If the plant is too dry we might have to water it two or three times. We don't always have to water the plant because it could also get water from rain in the spring. Sometimes we water the garden with a hose we water seeds, watermelon, tomato, strawberries, corn and other plants.

Sometimes people in the garden gets wet when their watering sometimes people trip and get wet they fall into a dirt that is muddy and sometimes they just get wet by the water when their watering. (Vachee)

What kind of water did they use? Did you use cold water? Did they use warm water? Or did they use hot water. Have you ever been in a garden? What do you know about garden? I have no idea what it would be like in a garden. But what I do know is you have to take good care of it unless you want it to die.

I am looking ford to being a gardener. I planted: carrots, watermelons, turnips, tomatoes, cantaloupe, and all the veggies that you can name. We made some veggie soup. I was the first to taste it was so, so good. I ate it all. (Danielle)

I saw a creepy crawly creature crawling up my hand. That creature made me want to get dirty! When you get dirty, it will usually be in the soil. The soil is usually wet because Jonesville waters the plants a lot during the spring. When the soil is dry that means that Jonesville needs to water the plants.

I have a lot of fun getting dirty because after you're done in the garden, you clean off your hands in freezing cold water!! Sometimes I get a drink from the water. Brrrr! When you're gardening, you don't want to wear sandals because tools could hit your feet or your foot could get stepped on. One day I was In the garden with my friend Aurelie. Both of us were working with Mr. Mike. He showed us how to sift the soil. We worked in the garden for about an hour! When Aurelie and I were done one of our hands were pitch brown!! Aurelie and I cleaned our hands in cold water, in the cold weather. (Harley)

starting up in the spring.

Every spring at Jonesville, we start our garden. When we start our garden, we plant the seeds. You have to cover it up with some soil. Then, you have to water it wont grow some times. You don't have to water it because the rain can water it for you, then the plant gets bigger. When you leave for summer break, the plant gets really big. Then, when you come back, the really big plant is still there, but when it gets colder, it starts to die. When it gets spring you plant all over again. And it gets really big again but some times it does not grow right because you don't plant it right some times you get dirty sometimes you are aloud to get a drink. (Jacob)

As soon as the weather warms up we all can start growing in the garden. We will all dig holes but we will not make them too deep because, well, I don't know why. Then, all of us will put seeds in the ground then bury them so they can grow. We also have to wait a year for them to grow so then they will be all done. Then when they are done we can eat all of the food in the garden. And when it is done we all can eat all kinds of food like strawberries and pota- toes and also some sunflower seeds. But when they are done we all have to pull the food out of the ground then we will get all dirty and then we have to wash of all of the food so we can eat it. Then when it is done we can make some salsa and lot and lots of other things too. (Damian)

It was winter. We planted peas. We watered the peas. They sprouted in the spring. They were beautiful; strawberries, sunflowers, pumpkins, and other things, too. They only were baby leaves and I liked them. Some were fuzzy and they felt funny. (Lakota)

When we talk about our garden I start to feel very frustrated because I never find out anything. I also feel scared a little bit because some people might laugh at me. Sometimes I feel silly because what I might say. I also feel very, very HAPPY! Because of what I do. Sometimes I feel bad a lot because when people say things that make me feel bad. Sometimes I go crazy because I am uncomfortable. After winter the garden looks like it is sad. (Danielle)

In the summer it was super hot everyday Monday through Friday was the day we worked in the garden and it was hot. And we would eat tomatoes and drink water from the faucet. And it was hysterical. We were laughing and joking. Sometimes we find bugs in the garden like for example grasshoppers. (Zandra)

strawberries.

Yesterday I discovered strawberries. The soil smelled nasty like wet mold smell. The wind blew in my face wane I adopted a strawberries flowers it was white, the peddles was sut.

When I go out there in the garden I see glorious dark green leaves. When I look very closely in side the leaves I see little yellow flowers growing out of it. I'm so excited because I can't wait until the strawberries grow. I also feel scared because maybe the little kids will pick the flowers from the plant. I smell the beautiful fresh air and the strawberry leaves are starting to smell

Jhnatton

like strawberries!! What I'm thinking and when I'm sketching I'm think-ing that when the strawberries grow I get to eat them.

One day while we were in the garden I found a strawberry plant. It was so small. Then a few months later, it was as tall as a pen. Then the next day for lunch we had the strawberries from the garden. They were big, fat, juicy, and tasty. They were gooood. If you don't like strawberries you don't know what your missing!!! Mmm. (slurp). Delicious.

While I was sketching I smelt the strawberry leaves when the wind blew. After I was done sketching the strawberry plants, I went over to the apple tree and I smelt a soft blossomy smell. While we were sketching I heard kids shouting giggling.

Yesterday afternoon I looked in the garden and I saw straw-berry's the first thing I thanked of was *"when are we going to eat the strawberry's"*. I was very satisfied that the strawberry was growing like it was supports too. And also was historical that is growing! It was sunshine was out too but it felt good with the wind. The smell was incredible. smelling the strawberries made me hun-gry for strawberries. And that is when told my friend Aurelie I will not bring a snack to school when the strawberries grow then on break Aurelie and me will eat the strawberries.

Our class went out to the garden to sketch things. I went to look at the patch of strawberry plants and I saw little strawberry blossoms and they looked like little tiny heads of lettuce. When I was outside on the ground I was worried that I was going to get my pants dirty and if I was drawing my picture well. When I finally started I could feel the cold crisp air on my face. I fell wile I was walking and I felt wet dirt. When I got up I could smell wet dirt. I felt surprised that the new school I was going to was growing strawberries.

the new greenhouse.

Imagine a little space with triangular tables pushed together where children sit with pencils and pieces of colored paper. They have just been told by taller children that a greenhouse will soon be built behind their school. The greenhouse is for them, an addition to their established garden. What would they say?

I know that Jonesville Elementary School is getting a greenhouse. I think it is going to be interesting in the greenhouse.

I wonder how the workers are going to make a greenhouse? I wonder if they are going to use wood or bark.

Are they going to color on the greenhouse? I think it will be red and green.

What are they putting in the greenhouse? Lattices and maybe roses and cherries.

I know that we'll have to kill the grass to make room for it.

We will plant seeds in the greenhouse and they grow all year long. And we will water them every couple days.

I know we are going to plant lots of different plants in it, like our cold weather plants. The greenhouse will keep the plants worm so they won't die.

It will be wet inside and Insects and bees will clam on our plants.

I predict that the Jonesville's greenhouse garden is going to look very good inside.

I will love it.

what we grow.

In the garden my class plants lots of kinds of vegetables. The vegetables we use for soup are potatoes, tomatoes, carrots, and more. We plant other vegetables for other foods. The classroom and Mr. Daniel, Mr. Mike and Ms. Thorp are growing peas and carrots and other things. The next day Ms. Small kicked a carrot over by accident and the carrot was a half of a carrot! It was empty in the middle. Ms Small found onions. She brushed the carrots off, and put them in the classroom. (Patrick)

These are deferent kinds of plants we grow in are garden. Sunflowers, daises, strawberries, dandelions, guess. (Frankie)

The kids ate tomatoes in June on Friday. And we dug carrots we took the sunflower seeds out of the stem. Sum of the kids ate the seeds. The seeds look black and Wight strip (D.J.)

I would feel nervous because it's my first time in the garden. I would also feel happy because I'd be excited to start planting. The kind of plants we plant are tomatoes, corn, carets and lots of different good stuff. When I'm in the garden I pick tons of stuff too like vegetables and fruit. I feel proud of my self because of the school and me. We really take care of our garden because we water the plants. (Aurlie)

Every year, we grow all different plants. This year, we are growing flowers, carrots, peas, radish, and onions because last year, we grew onions and we are still finding onions in the garden this year. At the end of fall, we pick the onions, carrots, peas, radish, and flowers because some of the plants that we grow do not like cold weather. Asparagus, for example, do like cold weather. So, we do not have to pick it until it grows. And not just us that work in the garden but the 1,2,3,4 and 5 work in the garden with Mrs. Thorp, Daniel and Mike we all is best friends in the garden. (Zandra)

I wish I could grow lots of plants in the Jonesville School gardens. I wish I could grow orange trees here but it is too cold in Michigan. I want to grow an apple tree at Jonesville. Apples taste good. I want to grow pear trees because they are one of my favorite fruits! They taste juicy. I wish we could have a spider plant because they look nice and they really look like a spider. I also like roses because I like red. I would like to grow them here. (Johnathan)

We picked tomatoes and we made soups for the community we watched ZOOM and we had pizza and pop and there was different pizzas there were pepperoni and cheese I got 5 of the pepperoni pizzas I was full and the next day we dig up potatoes and I accidently

slice the potatoes in half we left and the next day we went to school
we looked for more. (Lakota)

Here are some delicious foods Jonesville School grows.

Cucumbers,
Lettuce,
Tomatoes,
Potatoes,
Squash,
Pumpkins,
Corn,
Dill,
Carrots,
Asparagus,
Sunflower Seeds,
Strawberries,
Radishes,
and Sunflowers.

What a wonderful garden. Don't you think? Come and visit us and
we'll show you around! (Harley)

We dug up potatoes, and we picked tomatoes, too. We also picked corn. We saw a
mouse and crickets and caterpillars. We dug
up bugs and bug flesh, worms, and the worms
feel squishy. Carrots and strawberries grow in
the garden, too. Also, we saw creatures like
grasshoppers, bees, and roly-poly, and they
roll in your hand. We have flowers, too,
like marigolds and sunflowers. We pit corn
off the vine and ate tomatoes and some falled
on the ground and we helped Dan and
Mike pull sunflowers off the ground.

It was hard. We picked tomatoes off the pokey vine took pictures of the flowers that the first and second graders grew and I did a picture. (Lakota)

our dream cafeteria.

We wish that our cafeteria was different from the one we have now. The walls will be red with purple outlining and gold sparkles. We think we should have three classes at a time in the cafeteria. We would like round tables with light red cloth and purple seats with gold sparkles. Three classes would pick peaceful music and pick their flowers for their tables. We would have three medium aquariums with sharks, crabs, and fresh fish.

Our fancy dream cafeteria will have chefs and butler servers. The butler server would put our food on small silver trays. The students get to be chefs, too. They get to cook salsa, pizza, popcorn, and tamales. The food that the professional chefs would cook would be Chinese, chicken, steak, sushi, ribs, chicken salad, and Jersey Giants. Each month a class would plan the menu. We might like to have all-we-can-eat buffet.

our real cafeteria.

We eat in a cafeteria, which is a gym, when we are at school. A truck brings the food since they make the food in a factory. A person brings the food from the truck to the kitchen. We have seen them make food on TV but not here at Jonesville.

Mrs. Brown, the lunch lady, orders the food from the school district's factory at the middle school. She heats it up in a big oven. There are two trucks, one brings the milk and juices and another brings the hot-lunch and cold-lunch packs.

We eat in a cafeteria, which is a gym, when we eat at school. There are basketball hoops and an overhead screen about us. There is an echo and it is loud at lunch! Now there are 75 kids because the principal changed the lunchtimes. It was way too loud, almost every table was crowded and we could hardly sit at a table.

We sit on benches that are attached to the tables, three kids to a bench. They are very uncomfortable. They need cushions. We can sit wherever we want, but some of our friends don't eat with us. Some people throw food into the hoops.

ending in the fall.

In the fall we put the garden to bed for the winter. We made some corn stalks in the fall, we put the stalks in the front doors of the school. Some plants die in the fall. Some flowers will die in the fall.

So we pick the flowers to go to our grandmas and mom's. In the fall we harvest our vegetables. In October we pick pumpkins to turn into jack-o-lanters. We have to harvest everything up and dig everything up. We have to put away tools and the tomato cages. (Andrew)

The Garden
by Brenden

G is for green plants growing all around
A is for amazing animals hiding underground
R is for robin soaring overhead
D is for decoration all over the garden
E is for everyone working in the garden
N is for nature hiding everywhere.

CHAPTER SIX

A journey in one place.
written by Kristan Small, teacher, Jonesville Elementary School

Starting

I remember reading Farmer Boy *by Laura Ingalls Wilder when I was nine or ten years old. She writes about the childhood of her husband, Alanzo, as the son of a New York settler who worked a farm, raising various crops. In one chapter, Alanzo's father gives him a part of the family's kitchen garden for his own, to grow vegetables to take to the fair later in the summer. This is no small gift since the family's garden supplied much of their food and the cleared land was precious. Alanzo's goal was to grow the biggest pumpkin ever, and his father showed him how to "feed" a pumpkin bud with fresh cream through a wick in the spliced vine. I remember as a kid wanting to try that, looking for a Tupperware bowl that my mom wouldn't miss if I left it in the garden full of 1 percent homogenized milk. In the story, Alanzo visits the vine each day and tends to the cream wick. He listens carefully to his father's advice, not wanting to waste his opportunity. He works the soil, watches the rainfall, and wins first place at the county fair. I remember as a kid thinking, Alanzo's dad was just about the greatest adult ever for letting his son have his own garden space and helping him grow a giant pumpkin.*

I remembered this story soon after we started the Jonesville School garden.

We broke ground for the garden on a Tuesday, or maybe it was a Wednesday, twelve or thirteen years ago. There was nothing about the day that would mark it as a turning point or a special beginning. To find the actual date, I would have to revisit my ancient teacher's plan book, which I probably didn't consult much even when I was supposed to. What made the day important, however, was that it was late enough in the season for seeds to get started and early enough to see something happen to them before summer vacation took us all away from school. It was a nice spring morning, and we weren't going to spend it stuck in our classroom. That idea was a pleasant motivator for the students back then and has been ever since.

My teaching partner, Jan, and I were working on a unit about plants the spring we put the garden in. The learning objectives for the unit were crafted around a fraction of Michigan's expansive science curriculum. We planned to teach the children the parts of plants and their functions, the life cycle of plants, and surely, we could show the children photosynthesis, or at least its outcome.

At that time, the curriculum, or what children should know and be able to do and how they will show it, was massive in amount and elusive in meaning. Our state was just beginning to consolidate the knowledge of experts into curriculum documents that were meant to guide local school districts as they wrote their own local curriculum. Each district, with a team of teachers and others, would digest this state document into grade-level expectations for the teacher to use in the classroom as she made instructional decisions. That was what was supposed to happen. But as we waited for our district to make curriculum decisions, we went ahead and made some of our own.

The experts at the state level gave us broad statements about what fourth and fifth graders should already know about plants, and as a veteran of one or two years of teaching, I believed them. The experts made more pronouncements, vague at best, about what fourth and fifth graders needed to learn next about plants, and I believed that, too. Since our local school district had no real curriculum yet, Jan and I translated what we read in the state curriculum documents and wrote our unit.

We decided to make diagrams of plant parts, list all the things people use plants for, list all the plant parts we eat, dissect houseplants, learn photosynthesis, and observe plants in nature. All of this, since Jan and I embraced "hands-on-learning." We never thought to ask the kids what they knew or what they wanted to know. We never thought to question the age appropriateness of what the experts urged us to cover: What was too easy? What was beyond them? We had a perfect plan for what the kids would learn.

In some corner of the plant unit, we tucked a few lessons about plant-life cycle and I think it was at this point that I thought it would be fun and certainly hands-on for the kids to plant. We could put a few seeds into rinsed-out milk cartons along with a handful of dirt (I didn't use the word "soil" back then). We could watch what happened. I figured that since those seeds would likely turn into seedlings, we might as well dig up some playground sod and plant a garden. Jan agreed, as long as she got to oversee the diagramming and other indoor lessons and I led the gardening portion myself. Jan came from a southern farming family, and she had "been there, done that." The hands-on stuff was great as long as she didn't actually get dirty.

Heading up the garden portion of the unit was great with me. I was idealistic and energetic. My mom had always planted a few zucchini and tomato plants, and I had spent time in her little garden, probably trying to feed cream to a zucchini. But most years, when the plants didn't produce, we just got what we needed at the grocery store. I fancied myself to be earth friendly, a natural sort of person, even if I wasn't from real gardening stock. A garden would be a great little project for me to head up in the spring of my first or second year of teaching.

So we broke ground for the garden. We had no budget and didn't realize that eventually we might need one. The husband of a teaching assistant came that morning with a rototiller, and we pitched in to pay for the gasoline. A grandmother of one of the kids donated some seed packets to augment our spindly seedlings. No one wondered in advance if the tiller would actually cut the ignored sod and hard-packed clay underneath, and I am certain that we didn't ask permission to try it. No one checked germination dates on the donated seeds, and although we talked with the kids, we never once asked what they knew about gardens, what experiences they may have had. During our most important conversation with them, we explained that we would be working outside and starting a garden and that we would not be running all over as if it were recess. We would be learning about plants, after all.

We went out of the classroom, into the cool May air. The kids sat along what would become the garden's edge, in the dew ("Ms. Small, why is the grass all wet?") while I demonstrated how to use a stake and a protractor to start the garden's stringed boundaries. I realized, while nervously stabbing the hard earth, "This isn't the objective of the plant unit but an application of our geometry unit." We drove the stake in, we worked the rototiller, we later loosened dirt clods with shovels, and I thought again, "This isn't plant knowledge, but there are some examples of simple and complex machines out here." We found worms (I hadn't become a devoted vermicomposter yet); we uncovered beetle larvae. The kids debated whether to kill them by squishing, stomping, or hurtling. I think I startled them when I asked, "Why kill them at all?"

So the teacher was beginning to learn her lesson: A garden grows knowledge of its own, perfectly and naturally individualized for every student who steps inside it. Nature doesn't need a curriculum.

Changes

I remember the book The Secret Garden *by Francis Hodson Burnett. My dog-eared copy has soft green leaves and little pink flowers on the cover, with a drawing of a girl wearing a long wool coat—I always thought she looked like me. In the book, three children discover a tumbled, overgrown garden behind tall stone walls. They work together, in secret, to uncover the garden beds, the forgotten roses, the old fruit trees. They prune and till and mow and plant. They make changes, and they are changed.*

The following fall, the plants were bursting out of the boundaries of our new garden. There were sunflowers as tall as our classrooms, zinnias up to our hips, and tomatoes as big as our smallest students' faces. We had wisely chosen a protected corner where the gym and classrooms meet, in full sun and sheltered from storm winds. In the fall of our first harvest, we asked the principal for some money to buy camera film. We took lots of pictures—not just of the plants, but also of the kids' faces as they measured themselves against the huge results from the little seeds and the spindly greenish things they had planted only three months before. I have learned something: summer, which seems rather fleeting to me, is an eternity to the kids when they come back and see the garden in the fall.

The garden has become the perfect metaphor for schooling, since both are victims and celebrants of constant change. Nothing is ever the same in the garden two days in a row, and nothing stays the same in a school, either. The plants grow big, give up their beauty and food, die, and decompose. The soil itself has changed from clumped tan clay to rich black humus. The border has grown every year until the garden has more than doubled in size. When the kids go out to measure the garden's perimeter and area early in the spring, they can never agree: "Do we measure just the place that was planted last year or do we measure what is going to be planted this year, too?" The kids themselves grow taller, ask deeper questions, and lift bigger shovels—at least, the kids who stay at Jonesville School.

We lose about 30 percent of our students each year as they move from apartment to apartment, rental house to rental house. When Laurie, the Garden Lady, asks my fourth graders, "Who made salsa with me back in first grade?" only five kids respond. It is not uncommon for us to have fifth-grade students who have attended six different elementary schools— a different one for each year of schooling—and there are many students who move into my class after school has started in the fall and leave for somewhere else before the last day in June. With some families, the rate of movement is every three months—the time it takes for the first month's paid rent to pass, the second month's rent to become past due, and the eviction process to be completed. Stable housing is one of the factors that urban schools will never have in common with their suburban counter-parts. The effects of student transitions on the students themselves and the classrooms they leave behind are poorly understood, overtly ignored as "excuse making," and devastating to witness.

In the past several years, the administration at Jonesville School has changed dramatically as well. We have had seven principals in nine years, each with a different outlook and a different agenda. Some started the year with the best of intentions but by spring realized that there were better opportunities in other school districts, with perhaps fewer challenges. Others found themselves over their heads with a progressive staff, one that pushed hard to balance the ever-growing state curriculum with what was best for kids. We aimed to "de-institutionalize" schooling, and we didn't take no for an answer if the question was, "Is it good for kids?" My for-mer colleague Carol described us best when she said, "We can be led, but not misled."

Eventually, many teachers chose to leave, too. We lost three teachers in one year because of layoffs. Two had babies and decided not to return. Others retired, such as Betty who left early because she couldn't bear another year of changing and increasing mandates. She was tired of a target that keeps moving and gets harder to hit. Carol took a job coaching other teachers from a different building, and Gloria took a job with the state's Department of Education, training coaches like Carol. Currently, at Jonesville School there are only five out of twenty-five adults who have been there for more than four years. So while we are exasperated with how often our students move, we can guess what the families think of our staff turnover.

By far the greatest changes since we broke ground for the garden are the changes in the curriculum and standardized assessment. Back when we first planted seedlings, we were a multiage school, with teachers working together in teams, two classrooms, and at least a two-year range in the ages of our students. Our focus was developmentally appropriate learning, and we spent many years trying to interpret state and local curricula with that focus. We studied the literature of Jean Piaget and others who taught us to use what each could do as the best indicator of what the child should do next. But the days of each teacher balancing these state curriculum documents with the needs of their students or their desire to use a certain approach (Jan and I with our hands-on ideas), or of each teacher simply trusting a basal textbook, are over. Our state Department of Education finished writing the curriculum frameworks, which is still massive and now very detailed about student achievement at each grade level. There is an equally massive testing program to ensure that the curriculum is delivered in every classroom across the state. Students are sorted into "can do" and "can't do" groups based on test scores, and high school students who do well on their tests receive money toward college, even though test score and socioeconomic correlations tell us they are probably the least likely to need it. These state tests help identify at-risk students, and schools are rewarded, or sanctioned, depending on their overall "adequate yearly progress." The severest consequence for underperforming schools is that the state takes over such schools by reassigning teachers deemed "responsible for failure." Jonesville School is two years from that fate, if we do not change our test scores. It should be hard to plant fear in a place filled with passion and joy, but fear has been planted and is growing.

Owing to the high student transition rates, our local district interpreted the state curriculum into quarters; created a teaching calendar, or "pacing guide," for each grade in each of the core subjects; and attached its own massive testing program. Each teacher in our urban district is told very clearly what to teach, exactly when to teach it, and for how long. There are four tests, in mathematics, language arts, science, and social studies, four times a year and then we move on. Never mind if the students need more time or have more questions and want to extend their thinking. These local tests have two purposes. First, they are meant to create a system of teacher accountability: every teacher must teach the same thing at the same time or else the poor scores will reveal their failure to do so. Second, these tests are considered practice and predictors for success on the state-level tests.

We are not limited to just local and state curriculum standards and evaluation systems. Our students, like students everywhere, take the nationally normalized tests, such as the Metropolitan Achievement Test (MAT) and the Iowa Test of Basic Skills, and the scores from these tests are used to determine success or failure. Students take these tests every year, in all core subjects, and they are assigned a place on the bell curve. These tests help us meet the requirements of federal mandates such as the No Child Left Behind law, which is so complex that teachers and parents attend workshops in order to understand how it is to be applied to kids in classrooms. The one thing that *is* simple is this: real learning is now considered to be what is measured on paper-pencil tests. The belief that this form of accountability will help children learn is obsessive. Local tests prepare them for state tests, state tests satisfy national mandates, and national tests tell us that our urban children remain at the bottom of the bell curve. And young children carry the weight of all this, wondering when they can go outside and work in the garden again. In the beginning of the garden, I didn't realize how important it is to ask students what they want to learn, and now we are to believe there's no reason to do so.

One aftermath of the tightened curriculum and testing expectations, delineated by grade level, is that our multiage focus died a slow and painful death. We could no longer gather students of various ages to delve into a topic (such as plants), each student working at his or her own interest level and ability. We couldn't quantify the learning opportunities that arose among students, and we couldn't prove that each student learned their part of the pacing guide the year the school district said they should. We could *only* show what the kids did know, what they wanted to know, and what they could demonstrate they had learned. Our developmentally appropriate practices, such as insuring hands-on experiences during most of the day and using observation as the surest form of assessment, fell by the wayside as well. It seemed unfair to do too much hands-on, cooperative learning, when all of the testing is done on paper in silence.

The garden fell into disarray: there wasn't time to plant it or tend it carefully; plants and weeds equally grew tall. But it was there, with the brick walls of the gym and classrooms protecting it from the storm winds.

Harvest

Each of us enters the garden to gather nourishment, but it is not just actual fruit we take. We gather kernels of truth—lessons we have learned about ourselves and about the world that are the perfect fit for what we were seeking. The knowledge with which we leave the garden cannot be codified, cannot be assigned to a certain year in

our lives, and cannot be tested. The knowledge that the kids and I
scoop up is the real garden harvest.

The glaring truth about hunger is part of the knowledge that I gathered in the garden. I often bring fruit for class celebrations or leafy greens for "salad math," and whenever I do, the kids swarm around begging for one more slice or a larger serving. These kids are hungry. They are not getting enough food. I have always known that the majority of my students receive free or reduced-priced breakfasts and lunches at school. It is one of the factors in deciding which kids are at-risk, and our at-risk numbers are then used to decide how much money we receive from federal funds. The school, in many cases, is responsible for two-thirds of a child's nutrition.

I know that the federal meal program is connected to farm surpluses and that school lunch menus are built around what farmers have left over. The kids don't really like a lot of what is served to them and almost none of it is fresh. They have no choices to pick from and no way to pack their own lunches. They throw out a great deal of their school lunches (sixty-five pounds in one lunch hour) and are still hungry after lunch—perhaps test scores are actually hunger meters. The same size lunch that is served to a kindergartner is served to an adolescent fifth grader. The gym-cafeteria filled with these hungry children is on the other side of the wall where we began growing vegetables for a plant unit, and I finally understand the irony: children need to *consume* photosynthesis even before they can begin to learn about it.

Watching the kids munch veggies out of the garden, it's hard to ignore their craving for fresh, thoughtfully offered food and the integrity that comes with growing it themselves. "I like these tomatoes, Ms. Small, but I hate the ones at home" and "I don't eat salad, but I'll eat this salad." I have watched children making salsa and soup and realized for the first time what food really is: plants that people tend and grow. And while the children race through the cellophane-wrapped, processed school lunches, they linger over the little pizzas and pumpkin cookies that they make from their own garden produce. Awareness of hunger and the issues around feeding children are part of my gathered knowledge. But there is so much more.

Patrick comes to me one day after lunch. There were two big red and green strawberries in each lunch that day and the kids are really excited because they are growing strawberries, too. Patrick says that he wants to talk to me, and he seems to be really struggling with something. So once the kids are all quietly reading, Patrick, with his "language deficiency" and long pauses between words, asks me, "Do the taste come from the plant?"

I tell him I'm not sure what he wants to know. He says he had a strawberry at lunch and repeats, "Do the taste get made in the plant? Do it come from the plant?" He has discovered flavor and has decided to learn its origin. He feels his own curiosity becoming active and begins to form his own questions. He identifies me as a resource and starts to seek answers. Patrick begins his harvest.

Marcus turns around in his chair to face me; he sits in the chair nearest me so that I can have a calming effect on him. He has many challenges, including poor attendance and attention-deficiency/hyperactivity disorder severe enough to warrant a special education label and twice-a-day medication. Although we have just returned from lunch, he is munching on peanuts that he brought from home and his face looks thoughtful and full of questions. He pinches one half of a peanut in each hand, squinting at the tiny embryo on one of the halves, and he asks, "Is this a seed?" Before I can answer, he smiles broadly, as if he just discovered the joke I'd been playing on him all year, and he nearly shouts, "Peanuts are seeds! I just knew it!" Marcus is harvesting.

The class is brainstorming ideas for the writing we want to do about our garden. These ideas will become a plan to guide the writing process, from first drafts through published pieces, and I have posed these questions: "What should the world know about our garden? What do we want to tell?" The class breaks up into little discussion groups, and when we come back together to review all of the kids' proposals for writing topics, I grab a marker and begin to record them on a piece of poster-size paper. Someone wants to write about the peas we have just planted in the spring drizzle, a few kids want to record recipes for things we can eat from the garden, and others want to tell about digging. Then I call on Chen, who I must call on in order to hear him speak. He is so quiet, never sharing his thinking. After a long pause, which I always allow him, he says we could write about the bees, and the spiders, and the things in the garden that make us afraid. People around him nod their heads in agreement. Writing about our fears would be a good thing, indeed, and Chen begins a harvest for many of us in the room that day.

Kevin finds a baby toad in the garden where he often works during recess. He wants to hold it, and once he is holding it, he wants to cage it and keep it. Lots of other kids have gathered around and are reaching and grabbing for a chance to interact with this real live creature "from nature." I ask what we should do with the little toad, and they unanimously agree that a cage is needed, although they are not so sure that Kevin should be the one to keep it. I ask them what they will feed it and how they will make it cool at night and warm during the day with sunny places, like the garden, for the toad to sit in. I ask them, "Where can we get a cage as big as the toad's corner of the garden?" Someone suggests that maybe we should just leave the toad out there in his spot and maybe that's where he really belongs. We roll that idea around and adopt it: the toad stays and we leave. The kids are thinking differently about their right to control what they have power over.

When I look back at the pictures from the first year we harvested our tomatoes, pumpkins, and sunflowers, I am so young and I know so little about teaching and learning and the children in my care. I used to be so sure that as a teacher, I would either have all of the answers or I would know where to find them. In those old photos, I have that look of complete (and premature) confidence as I enact plant units on children. There is no sign of the weariness with the education industry that I sometimes feel now.

I don't teach predetermined units in the garden anymore; I just garden with kids. And when I do, there are thousands of moments of pure curiosity, when the kids seek out knowledge from me, from one another, and from what they are experiencing. "Why are the grubs see-through?" "Why is the sun in my eyes 'cause it wasn't when we started"? "Why won't my mom let me drink out of the hose at home?" They seek out knowledge because they want to *have* it, not because they have to *do* anything with it or prove it.

We defy the unspoken guideline that gardening time is too uncontrolled and too uncontrollable to meet curriculum demands. We water and plant and pluck and stake, but not because some teacher's book says to. The garden lets us know what needs to be done, and the kids are eager listeners when it is their little plot of land that is doing the telling.

Place

We dig dirt
We shove mud
We toss weeds
We worm love

We measure edges
We count seeds
We gage angles
We voice needs

We thank heaven
We thank earth
We dig deeper
We soil birth

We plant rows
We paint signs
We build a garden
We grow in kind

We trade seedlings
We revel in stalks
We pet petals
We plant talk

We are kids
We are youth
We are the people
Who inherit the earth.

The garden is a beginning and a starting point. It is the perfect symbol of constant, chaotic change. It is where we create our own learning and gather new knowledge. But really, the garden is just a little place in the back of an elementary school.

Like any place that a person is able to visit again and again, over some span of time, it can be used to measure change. The kids who stay a year feel the change of fall to winter to spring—they have this place to look at again and again and it invites the question, "What has changed?" The kids who stay a few years can feel when they have finally grown taller than the tomato plants and are able to reach the corn at harvest time. Their sense of their own growth is present on the mulched pathways. When I look around in the garden, I measure myself against the pear trees. They are taller and bigger around now, and they are finally bearing fruit. They measure time and my movement through it. Standing in the garden, visiting the same place again and again, I can feel what I know now layered over the limited ideals of that young teacher. In the last line of his poem where he spells out GARDEN, Brenden writes, "N is for Nature hiding everywhere." Perhaps it is our own human nature that hides right in front of us if we don't have a place like the garden to keep measuring ourselves with.

SEVEN

The pizza-Earth reunification.

written by Daniel Brooks,
university student volunteer

7 Feb 2002 welcome to the politics of Lewiston

Arrived at the coffee shop at 8:20 a.m. or so; Dr. Thorp came a little later. I haven't a clue what we said to each other because my body was still confused about the whole "being awake and not writing a paper at 8:00 a.m." thing. So we drove to Jonesville; past the dump, some small and large residences, trailer homes, and rolling hills. When the road gets higher you can see the highway to your right, and there was an old Michigan History sign announcing our arrival to J-ville next to an old barn or something— you could still feel the presence of the highway. *I'm sure they can't see stars up here*. This bothers me. If you live in a poor area, or you're a farmer (or a city kid bused out from home), you should be able to see the stars at least when you gaze up at night. All of the stars, not this light-polluted bullshit; I mean the Milky Way, cotton-swabbed across the sky like sand on the beach kind of stars.

Dr. Thorp and I arrived at the school, and it looked like any other school to me. When we went in I felt out of place, as if my mom should be there, as if I was going into *my* elementary school late and my mom was taking me to class. I really missed her right then, so I told Dr. Thorp that these kids probably think that she is my mother, which was really just what I was thinking. I'm not sure why I termed it that way, but I was uncomfortable there and, for some reason, suddenly wanted to make a good impression on the ole Doc. Probably a good twenty or thirty years older than me, Dr. Thorp (Laurie) had a quick pace as we rushed through the school. Tall and thin, her short wispy red-blond hair bouncing along, she always seemed a little hyper, especially from about ten paces ahead.

Walking down a long hall, feeling like I needed a hall pass, we walked past this kid, John, with a bowl haircut and a dark T-shirt. He looked at Laurie then at me, did a kind of jaw dropping double take as we passed, then looked right at me and said, "Wooohh! Did your hair go through a tornado?!" I responded with something like, "yeah you're totally right," and laughed, exchanging looks and smiles with Laurie. We went into her sister-in-law's classroom and dropped off our coats. Laurie talked with the kids for a second, telling them something about what we were about to do. I wasn't paying attention; I was looking at the kids and all their multiracial wonder; at the classroom, the plants, and pictures (it seemed ten little Jackson Pollocks were before me); at the teacher, how she and Laurie talked to the kids, overemphasizing everything. The kids were moving around a lot, touching one another, falling over, being small, looking around, being huge; looking out the window, the door, at the ceiling; craning their necks all the way. Every one of them wanted to do everything all the time, hands raised, wondering. The educators always ask: What happens to this? What happens to this thirst for learning?

While Laurie and the teacher were talking, some of the kids were stealing glances at me. I smiled and waved, they gave me momentary looks, some giggles—a justified present after the tornado and all. I was probably introduced, but the kids simply weren't listening; so looking giant and old, we went to another classroom across the hall. Laurie talked for a minute, then introduced me; I felt really important, and all the kids were wondering who I was. Whispering, they looked older, moved around less, seemed more attentive, more interested. Laurie seemed to know every kid's fucking name, which blew me away, but she'd been going there for a while.

The second room was bright, lit by the G-d awful fluorescents (even on a sunny day). This teacher told kids to stop fidgeting, she TOLD them. What power. Laurie was describing what we were going to do, asking the kids, "How do you make a pizza? Have any of you ever made pizza with your families?" I noticed later that no one at Jonesville School said "mommies and daddies," they always said families. I remembered that in poor, jobless households, suicide rates are higher, so are abuse rates and divorce rates; I stood in front of thirty-plus pie charts and bar graphs, learning how to make a pizza. It seemed so bright in there; I later dreamed about it, the teacher in that room and her lights.

I really hate fluorescent lights.

What was great about that moment was the way Laurie was talking—still overemphasizing, but a little differently. (It struck me later that she talks to our class the same way she talked to those kids. I find nothing wrong with this, I like it; she keeps my attention pretty well.) So, we learned about the pizza-stuff creation, about how food comes from the earth, the sun, and all that. The kids had grown some wheat (flour) which we were now turning into pizza. All that said, we returned to the first classroom with younger kids. Feeling more confident, I sat closer to the kids this time, some of them noticed me, but most listened to Laurie's sister-in-law read. The room was much more comfortable as the shit lights were off and every window open so the sun shone in. And they were all *swaying,* intimately swaying to some silent rhythm, together. The sway was like water, back and forth, back and forth, each agent the key to his or her own individual movement, but all were together—swaying. They were still touching one another all over, almost sexually, no, more animal-like, laying all over one another (like tigers), looking around, moving, moving, moving together, stuck in this ocean of sound from the mouth of the woman in the front of the room; back and forth, back and forth . . .

I started to sway, thinking of a melody by the composer Erik Satie, "Gymnopédie No. 1." Strange how long a moment lasts, because we swayed for hours, back and forth, back and forth. The last time I swayed like this was at a friend's funeral, or with my girlfriend, standing in her mother's house, hugging her swaying, or with my father, or mother, or just with sudden joy, all this makes you want to *move*. Sometimes, watching the clouds on my back, I start to sway with the Earth: it feels as if I'm on the side of a great and ancient thing, part of a four-billion-year-old dance in space-time. The children and I were dancing.

So I decided to play a larger role and asked the kids where wheat comes from. They looked to their teacher thinking, "who is this strange man?" She asked them something and twenty-or-so hands shot up, swaying.

We went to make the pizzas, filtering through the two classes of kids. Laurie told me some background on most of them, a series of statistics shoveled through our four chairs: fatherless, motherless, broken homes, poor, abandoned, rapes, beatings, smiling and dirty with whatever amount of wheat I could get on to them. I set up the table, Laurie returned, and we began making pizza with kids again. I was getting more and more comfortable, moving kids along, chatting. But 11:30 a.m. had rolled around, and I had to leave. I drove home feeling okay, covered in wheat dust.

I think I didn't take any notes in Calculus that day.

19 Feb 2002 elephants, living rooms

On Mike's first day, we got lost driving to Jonesville. Wandered around a few Lewiston neighborhoods, some of 'em were nice. Some weren't. It struck me that there will be days when your heart explodes because the kids don't understand (yet) how shitty their lot is. Some may never figure it out; but now we've got 'em. We'll teach them with every ounce we have to live and enjoy life for what it is; if we could only find our way out of this fucking subdivision.

Mike has a mind of his own, is sick of bullshit, and is ready and willing to laugh at absurdity (though sometimes it's hard). He has a sly smile and disheveled brown hair, a neat kid I'd like to befriend; we're both a little apprehensive about all this "going to help out in an elementary school" stuff. The school still looked like an elementary school, and now with passes in hand, at least I felt surer of things. The school secretary (a light-haired woman with a singsongy voice whose multitasking ability is amazing) wore huge glasses, and uncomfortably she had us sign in. She told us to go to Mrs. P's room. Mrs. P was probably in her mid-forties, with possibly curly hair, pulled back and in a bun, and she *looked* like a second-grade teacher, slightly plump with a commanding voice. As we entered, she told us to put our coats in a metal closet next to the door. Mike and I realized that as far as the kids are concerned, we're teachers. Our outer garments had disappeared into the world of adulthood with a metal clang. Mrs. P sat down and started talking to the kids, they keep turning around and looking at us, whispering things; Mike and I were being judged, sized up: Who are we? Why are we here? If I could know what goes around in a child's mind, there I'd find the wonder and joy of living amazement, what is? what is? what is?

The boy I thought was from another school, a second grader named Ricky, sat at a computer playing some kind of game. I don't remember if I talked to him right then or not, but we didn't make eye contact. I had been assigned to help him read and we were both unsure of ourselves. Mike was assigned to Timmy, and I to Ricky, brown skin, brown eyes, a keen smile. He found a book he'd read before, and we went out in the hall. Timmy was a small white boy, and he took to Mike instantly. Ricky wasn't so sure about me, he just stared down at the closed book, so I tried asking him about what he likes to do, if he likes this particular book, anything. No response, then without looking at me he started to read in a jumpy fashion, up and down, his mind's motions all over the book, he skipped words and pages; he just wanted to get it over with. But I wouldn't let him, he grew annoyed with me: "Who is this strange man asking me to say 'because' over and over? What right does he have to tell me anything?"

We finished the book, and got up. Once back in the room, Mrs. P told us to pick some games and play with the kids. So we played games, I with Carmen with her enormous glasses and magnified eyes and Jay with his short hair and easy smile. An Asian boy, Sam, kind of played with us, he and Jay wore the same outfit, and the two seemed good friends; no leader among them, they just enjoyed one another. Mrs. P told Mike and I in between games that the kids fight a great deal while playing games because they don't get enough attention and one-on-one time at home so they don't understand games very well. They don't know how to play because their parents aren't around enough.

At the end of game time or whatever it was, a lot of the kids disappeared; those who stayed sort of found little things to do, I found myself drawing with Alison, Ariel, Tess, and a boy named Dan. Alison is a white girl with a loud voice; she's a little pudgy with brown eyes and shoulder-length brown hair. Tess has long hair and dimples; she has a few teeth missing and is very quiet. She has the air of someone who will one day be quite intelligent, and I hope she develops her own voice. For now she's quiet, but there is a shine to her, I feel as if she knows something. Ariel is a black girl with a grand smile, usually her hair is in tight braids with some sticking up in the front; like Tess, there's something about her I can't place. It seems purposely hidden (I can't help the images of her forebears hiding something from their masters). I feel as if it's an ancient *strange* knowledge like that of the Jewish women I grew up with. (I wonder what affect hundreds or thousands of years of oppression have on a culture.) Toothless Dan, a sweet boy who has managed to be friends with the girls, has a flat face with a few freckles here and there. I drew a moonscape and told the kids about the constellations I was going to insert; I don't recall what they were drawing (though I wish I did). They all sat as close to me as possible though I was shvitzing a little from the heat of the room; it was nice to sit down for a minute.

11:30 a.m. again reared its ugly head and Philosophy of Ethics beckoned. Off to college.

Mike and I drove home trading stories, trying to write down the day's events.

12 Mar 2002 Mike and I own the school

I had been dating my friend Annie Lefkowtiz. She teaches four different classes for her education program at Oakland University and has won every award there, literally. She carried the dream for Martin Luther King (I suppose it got heavy after the FBI, Mafia, Cubans, Republicans, CIA,

Germans, KKK, and everyone else who rode a bullet into the beginning and end of an era in American civil life)—an award for helping African American communities. She will prod you with huge brown eyes and an unequaled passion to fight for the life of the voiceless poor, so I showed her how everything is interrelated and so endless and endless and endless and she reminded me that the poor youth,

>   have
>   the
>   smallest voices
>   and
>   the loudest
>   need.

Bruce. Bruce is an interesting boy. He has a large face with huge eyes, normal little boy's hair, and says the funniest things. He is going to be a great class clown, politician, or lawyer—why the hell am I writing this for? He is what he is, a child. A child with bright eyes who is nothing more than the infinity of his imagination: I'm sorry to have tried to box him in. Anyhow, Bruce is incredibly funny, and we did math. He had a hard time remembering things without a prompt from these little boxes that represented ones, tens, and hundreds. He kept getting flabbergasted when he got it right, looking up at me, "How did the boxes know?!"

Later, I was counting boxes with Ariel, Tanisha (she and Tanisha are the only black girls in the class), and a blond-haired white girl whose name I cannot recall. The two black girls generally stick together and enjoy mimicking the loud, strong, no-nonsense hand-in-the-face attitude of black women popularized by TV culture. The white girl seems preoccupied by the task at hand, while the other two are preoccupied with arguing. Sitting with these girls, I wonder about their futures and those of the rest of the class. Is Carmen going to become pregnant at fourteen or fifteen or even thirteen? Sometimes I can't help but see in them the personality traits from the community I grew up in. Who is going to go to college for free, or be on financial aid, or going to college at all? Most of all, who is going to be like my ageless and buried friends? In my freshman year of high school, we were told that on average one student per graduating class dies before graduation; we lost two. I can't help but look around this classroom and wonder. I suppose I have some ghosts in my mind that won't fade. These kids are young, they have no use for the future.

dayless moments; the things you forget to write down but stick somehow to the meat of your mind, or were lost because you wrote them in this little ass notebook that falls apart all the time

I went alone to the school during spring break, I couldn't get a hold of Mike. Timmy told me that day he had to move, but he said he'd still go to Jonesville. He said his stepfather (I think) and mother were having troubles with something, but to me it sounded like money. I remember thinking about how the cheap housing in Lewiston isn't so, and Timmy's parents were going to move pretty far away because, again, of what sounded like money issues. I think he said something about rent for the house, I couldn't exactly tell, but something seemed awry. I remember that day was rainy and warm for March. The boys were acting up, and I noticed for the first time how the girls are much quieter than the boys. How much sexist crap is crammed into our heads by the time that we're eight or so? A lot I assume. I remembered thinking one way about girls and another about boys before we learned what made girls, girls.

Timmy was very subdued that day. His eyes were sunken and he looked old, not old like twelve but old like forty, his glasses reflected more light than normal, and the joy had drained from his face altogether. I almost wanted to avoid this joyless child, older than I was. I already knew this day would wear on me.

Mrs. P asked if I would read with Ricky, of course yes. We went to the library. But he didn't want to read, he wanted to escape.

"Do you have a car, Mr. Daniel?"

"Yeah, kinda, it's my brother's. I bought it from him for a dollar."

"Really! Where is it?"

"We can't see it from here, it's behind that thing someone calls a car."

It was behind an Excursion/Expedition/Suburban/whatever from the late nineties.

"It's an old car but it gets me to those far places I convince myself I need to get to."

"Take me to McDonald's, Mr. Daniel!"

"No, Ricky! Why don't we just read this real quick and then talk for a minute?"

This outburst seemed sudden, as if he was afraid to say but it just had to come out.

"Why do you want to leave school?" I asked after a moment's thought.

"I don't like it here." He said to the window, to the rain.

"I love school, I go to your school and my school, in fact my school is on break and I still felt like coming to your school." I said to the side of his face.

The book we were trying to get though was dull and repetitive; Ricky had a hard time with the words, as most of them were made-up-sound words. Nothing in it was all that interesting to a twenty-first century TV child.

"Why don't we just leave? Just take me to McDonald's!"

"Why do want to leave Jonesville? Mrs. P is such a great teacher. And all your friends?"

I almost said, *you have no idea how much we'd all like to take you away from here, not school though.* But he wouldn't have understood the metaphor. He didn't answer my real question. He got up and walked around saying nothing I can remember. He started playing with the old Dewey drawers and pulled out some rods that keep the cards in order.

"Ricky, what are you doing?" I didn't yell, I know I didn't because I had read about this kind of thing the day before; and for some reason, I wanted to break things right then, too. I don't know why, but we shared the emotion and he'll never know it. I took it out on my car later though, drove like a maniac. Ricky turned around and ran to the book checkout, "watch this," he said. I watched, he checked out a book, he tried hitting buttons, and I walked over and picked him up and plopped him down in front of the book.

"What are you doing? This isn't fun, Ricky, stop it."

He didn't. He kept doing things and ignoring me, so I told him I was leaving. I didn't know what to do. I realized he had problems, and I didn't want to further anything. I thought I'd just take him to the principal. I got up and walked out. He ran out after me, crying. Fuck, I made an awesome little kid cry. I remembered thinking, *I'm human, I'm a person, there's no fucking book written on Ricky, I know this kid, so I can help.* I turned around.

"No, Mr. Daniel! I'm sorry! I'm sorry!" tears streaming, eyes ablaze.

"Are you going to break things in the library, are you going to mess with the computer?"

"No." Looking at the ground.

"Are you going to read?"

"Yes." Looking at the ground.

"You realize you may have done things in there that could get *us* in a great deal of trouble." He looked up when I said "us." "I am going to have to tell someone about what you did because it would be dishonest not to. So long as you don't misbehave anymore, I'll be sure that you don't get in trouble. If you misbehave anymore, I am leaving. I really like you, Ricky, but you hurt my feelings." (There are probably a million things that I didn't record in this thing about Ricky and I interacting, but he had never done anything before that really made me mad, and this case hurt as well. Why did he do those things in the library? What is going on in his life that makes him so mad? He wanted me to be mad at him, what does he want to draw my attention away from or to and why? I suppose those questions can never be answered unless I follow him home like a ghost and see what's going on. But as I said, there's no book on Ricky.)

We sat back down, both drained. I read the made-up words, realizing that he is in second grade and these words aren't even real. I don't know what kids in second grade, let alone those with reading problems, are expected to have read. We started moving along, but he still didn't get the pattern to the made-up words. Eventually we left, and I took him back to Mrs. P. I returned the things Ricky had misplaced to the secretary after trying uselessly to put them back together. She promised to make sure he wouldn't get in trouble, which seemed a measure of faith in me by her. I probably shouldn't be making agreements with seven-year-olds, but why not treat him like a person? I told Mrs. P about it a little, and all the kids wanted to read with me, but I just wanted to leave.

At some point, the rain had stopped. It was still nice out, but a little chilly. I got in my car and screamed. I've always felt emotionless, I don't really know why: probably TV, or media in general (too much gore), or something in my youth I don't recall; so that could be going on. Here, inside the car, was the scream of a confused man. These kids have so many problems; are they all social problems? Ricky's mystery and Timmy's plight. They're the two kids who act up the most—this is so obvious and insane. That's why Mike and I were told to watch them, but all the kids seem in need—Carmen, Jesse, Bruce, Angel—I suppose I could think of any kid and something that bothers me about them would come up. Some days are just fun as hell, no, most days are; but then there are these moments, screaming at a steering wheel. Ricky is so mad, *so mad*, there's no one out to get him, but he is attacking the world. Timmy is the same, they are both so lost, they know something is wrong but can only regurgitate little bits and pieces. And it is all social, societal, cultural; the fault of gigantic human gears and events that necessitate the need for them to remain stupid and poor so they can make a little money and buy a lot of crap; and hate what and who they should and love war, and cars, and God, and hope for death because in death is freedom; the promised land is gun-shot, wrist slit, pill away; it's heroin, coke, meth, and E (ecstasy); and fuck-ing most of all, alcohol. Freedom is everywhere but it'll cost you; we need you to make our cars, our TVs, our DVDs, our PlayStations, our univer-sity dinners; we need you to clean our university community bathrooms, we need you to read my complaints about your jobs; I fucking need you to swipe my goddamned credit card so I can fill up my car and drive to your elementary school and teach you to read so you can tell the differ-ence when I ask for Marlboro or Camel because I need my morning smoke before work.

I turned on my car. Clutch down, key forward.

Flying down the road and over the highway, sunroof open, windows down, I reach fifth gear probably faster then my car was made to. What I wanted was to cry, *social reproduction, social reproduction*, I kept thinking, *it's not your fault, you just want to live, no one can help how things are, only what they will be.* I drove the long way home listening to the wind. I started to feel better, watching the fields pass. I turned on my tape player and fast-forwarded to a song by Godspeed You Black Emperor! "Lift Your Skinny Fists like Antennas to Heaven." It has no lyrics, but the trumpets do tell one hell of tale.

It starts with a slow, cautious, build. A lone trumpet wakes to the sound of a gently strumming guitar, another instrument joins with each measure, a new sound, eventually another trumpet wakes, the build gains, a violin joins, and another, you can feel an undercurrent of anticipation *building*, oozing over your being, and for some reason you feel afraid, you look cautiously out (like a child), and a door opens in your mind some-where, you smile, and

boom

the horns rush over the cymbals (crash, crash, crash), they build as the anticipation and the fear blend into this new hope like white to black but you're too busy listening to the fists screaming toward the sky, higher, higher, higher, screaming in delight, moaning in delight, you're watching the fists as they rise (why?), they reach up, the hands open, the band plays, we run for the fists, white to black to brown covered in earth, we bury the seeds, we wait for rain, we gather the rain, we drink the rain, we scream again, our lungs open, we breathe the dirt, the rain pours and we bury the seeds with our hoes, our shovels, we eat like people do, fists raised gloriously enraged with a new knowledge of life, never lost, never bored,

and it passes
or returns, but we
are calm
like
seasons
and no matter how lost I get in that song, Ricky is still
    going home hungry.

20 Mar 2002 the Thorp returns

I was so tired that day, I know from the many pictures we took that day; I can feel it from the pictures. We first went to lunch, Laurie giving me two small compost pails, one of which Timmy immediately took. He ran around asking kids to throw compostable food (carrots, that day) into the pail. With a squadron of children at my heels, I wandered around the room with my own pail, eating most of the carrots. Honestly, I was annoyed by the million kids following me, some were rude and one had a rather strange quirk. He kept trying to punch me in the balls, which I didn't really like and luckily could block easily as his fist always flew back, before doing it. Carl, from Mrs. C's class: Small, short, blond kid with a strong voice. Those in my entourage started to fight me for the damned pail, grabbing it and throwing anything into it they could pick up. They all fought over that pail, and I found myself worried about Timmy, but it was me they wanted.

Lunch, with little to say, ended, and a few kids and I went with Laurie to dump the compost outside. Sandrina, Carmen, Stephanie, another girl whose name I never learned went out into the world to dump compost. Carmen had to be held, laughing as she does, I cannot describe. We watched the carrots fall into the bin, and Laurie told us about consumers or some such thing.

You know when you look at certain people how you remember a thing about them that they or someone else told you. The memory floats around while you interact with the person, and may even inhibit things you want to say or what you think you can say. There is Stephanie. A tiny-eyed, fragile girl, she has a small face and the laugh of a women eight times her age. I will never understand the realm of her life nor her afflictions; there were things to be explained, there will always be a level that only she and her family can understand, well hidden like the shadows of her father. A beautiful child, burdened with an ugly family history, she is rarely in school, as whatever takes her away brings home a world of sorrow known to few. Having been told that she may not live long, I am now among the hundreds who wonder: *I hope Stephanie is in school tomorrow.* When I look at her, I always see moments of that conversation over lunch when she revealed her illness to me, and as such I hope she'll be in school tomorrow.

We made Thundercakes today out of overripe tomatoes, a recipe found in the children's book some of the teachers read at the school a few months ago, and a food that actually exists according to my Marxist professor (he told us they were made by his grandmother years ago). Mike and I set up some tables, taught ourselves the recipe, and went to it. The kids all wanted to do everything, it was hard dividing them up to do so, and I wanted to do it well as this was my first time working in Mrs. C's class. I was given Brad, Michelle, and a girl in a flowery dress. Brad is in constant need of my attention, though because of another sleepless night I'm feeling a bit under the weather. I put too much of an ingredient in the bowl when time was running out; I remember telling Laurie about it, feeling like my soul was dry; I thought I was dead. I had wasted the flour the kids had made from their stone-ground wheat; I had ruined the plan for the day and perhaps used the rest of the cocoa and she laughed about it, "Ohhh don't worry . . . ," lifting my spirit. The kids and I quickly made another batch, then set to another. A second batch of children started out, and Ariel at Mike's table discovered that not only could we eat the goop we had all made (which I admit that WE ALL had been doing; Mike and I aren't quite the positive role models), but also we could place the said goop on Mike's face. I gave Stephanie my camera, and many funny-as-hell shots were taken of the Michael de-cleanification process. A bunch of hands stormed his face. It was great, but I had to keep my group rolling as we were transferring our goop from bowl to cupcake tins.

At cleanup time, the little buffoons were unsure where to put the excess flour on the table, so they decided my hair was the best storage spot. As Mike and Laurie left, pairs of hands found their way to my head and placed as much of whatever was on the tables into my hair. (According to Michael, I looked like Rob Zombie, I thought he looked like a guy covered in goop. Life is indeed good even if war rages everywhere according to my Marx professor.) Sometime during all this, Mrs. P floated in, sing-songy voice, commanding presence, and all. It nearing 3:00 p.m. and my Marx class rolling toward me like a million bricks of college boredom. Mrs. P sat at this large board and with the kids wrote a huge excuse letter to my prof. for being late. After some time, Mike and Laurie returned; the teachers had turned off the lights, and the kids and I were all lying on the floor. The student teacher was reading to us. And to solve a mystery, yes I was fast asleep. Before leaving, Mike and I each had a Thundercake, and they were chunky (like our hair).

I went to my Marx class and delivered the letter, Dr. Calfana and the cute girl in the front thought it was great. No one else did. Calfana started ranting about the connectivity of helping kids and Marxist thought. I slunk into a plastic chair and took out my notebook, with the perfect appearance of attention on my face, and the perfect, complete, and utter abandon of reality in my mind. I got home that day and wrote a poem, the first in a long, long, long time. It's about my older sisters, two infinite women.

27 Mar 2002 didyouknowdidyouknowdid youknowdidyouknowdidyouknowdidyou?

I always seem to forget that freedom comes in ready-made packages, without instructions, called babies. And as such I always forget that it's the fault of every generation that the next is so fucked up. I suppose that's a dive into the nature-versus-nurture problem . . . Are all of our most ancient of questions so hard to comprehend that it seems there is no way to understand them? If you fill a kid's head with crap, you'll have a crappy kid. Pretty simple, right? Whether legitimate or not, I'm making the argument that we don't give most of our kids a chance. We fill them with chemicals (fast food) and give them a below-par education while starving them half the time.

Anyhow, outside today was a tug-of-war and some basketball. We did a lot of recording with the camera, pictures, and all. At lunch, I was thoroughly surprised to see the amount of trash thrown away; I taped it. Amazing how plastic the food looks. As usual, the kids gave samples away, even more amazing is what it tastes like. It is pretty cool how they get salt to look like odd-colored chicken and beef in dinosaur shapes. I wonder if there was someone in a corporation one day with an epiphany: "Hey, let's make food look like . . . stuff! We can sell it cheap to poorer school districts!" What the hell were they thinking?

Before leaving, Mike, Laurie, and I brought some of the hands and eyes and wonder out to the garden where Laurie used her be-interested voice, and as always we were.

24 Apr 2002

While doing our final editing on the video, Mike and I both remarked how this experience has really changed how we view ourselves and our world. It's strange to know you're experiencing a time that is changing and will further change your entire person. We arrived and went to lunch with Mrs. P's class, they were really hyper and jumpy, wonderful. Once in the lunchroom, Natale, a girl with whom I had interacted a good deal but never recorded, walked up to Mike and I, standing and watching the kids in line.

Kind of secretly she said, "I hate this food."

"Why?" one of us said. Looks exchanged.

"'cause . . ."

"Why do you hate the food?" Mike asked.

She looked at us as if we were out of our minds, "because it's just cheese!" She ran off. Huh? Just cheese? Sure enough, as I sat with Carmen and a few others as promised earlier, all around me were (not eating their apples) eating two bread sticks glued together by and filled with cheese. After some discussion and interaction about lunch, the kids filed out of the gym to the playground, and I went to sit with Stephanie and a few others who were still eating. We got into a conversation about some girl who was no longer her friend. When Carmen came to join us, Stephanie gave me a bag of bread sticks to eat. They wanted to see what I thought of the food. The bag was warm and on its cover was written something most of the school couldn't read with an exclamation point. Whatever it said, it did it with emphasis. As the two watched in anticipation, I took a lactose pill and began eating the grease thing. I don't remember this being on the food pyramid. Stephanie and Carmen told me I had to eat the whole thing, "it was bad to waste food," Stephanie said. I feel like they wanted to test me: *Can he eat the crap?* Stephanie nonchalantly asked me why I had to take a pill, I explained to her that my body can't digest dairy products. She started telling me that she has to take a lot of pills every night, then she opened her tiny eyes wide, as if amazed at what she was about to say, "I have very, very, very bad kidney problems." A four-fingered hand then pulled part of her shirt down relieving a calloused cracked skin and a large tube with white hospital tape around it protruding from her chest. She looked up at me, proud, and *aware* of it. Like many kids here, she momentarily seemed far older than I was.

The conversation changed quickly. What Stephanie had shared was a part of her like toes or laughter, and I needed time to digest it. Stephanie is still a great unknown. We finished eating, and I swallowed a few lumps in my throat, and I left them there before going outside. Sometimes part of the job of any person involved in a school (such as this) seemed to be to shut the fuck up and stave off your worry for later.

During the hectic interim when Mrs. C's kids arrived, Alison kept mouthing for me to "ask her, ask her, ask her" about reading with Alison. I had told Alison earlier that we'd have to put it off; she didn't care. Mrs. P was reading *Mohammed Moves the Mountain*. A great book. Caleb, one of Mrs. C's first graders, announced that it is easy to move a mountain, all you need are cranes and bulldozers. After that comment, it was as if Mrs. P was reading it to him with the rest of the class listening. Laurie arrived and had the kids vote on what vegetables would be in the garden this summer. "You're a garden god!" one kid said aloud when she sat down, another corrected, "She's a Garden Lady!" Otherwise, the kids were all attentive. As the lesson ended, Mike and I said our good-byes and left.

the summer after

When classes ended in May, Laurie found a grant to pay a student to work at Jonesville School. I needed a job and e-mailed a few thousand people. Laurie responded, and I found myself getting paid to garden with the kids. Problem is I'd never gardened before, so she loaded me with books on gardening and composting and worm bins.

Not much happened in the garden. I mostly spent those days talking with the kids and pulling weeds; we planted some vegetables, and watered a great deal; I did some odds and ends for the teachers, chatted with the janitors and the lunch staff, and steered clear of the gym instructor who didn't seem to like me. I think it's because I wore a woman's gardening hat out there, and he always gave me weird looks when I was cajoling around in that hat. I imagine him looking at me thinking, "Ah, that damn ninny again . . . ", or was it that I sent the kids in with muddy shoes through the gym, "Ah, that damn ninny's done messing up the floor again . . . "

I spent a good month or so going to Jonesville a few times a week. Taking kids out of their classrooms and into the small plot of land outside the gym-lunchroom. By the time the last day of school came around, no one would flat out say, "What the hell have you been doing out here? Where's the vegetables?" You send a philosophy major out to do a gardener's job, you'll get a bunch of kids wondering about the existence of the self and personal decision, not to mention a tiny garden. Descartes died not because of old age, but because some queen had him waking up at 6:00 a.m. every day when the man never bedded earlier than 3:00 a.m. or so; unlike that religious cryptic, I plan to change my habits. I would learn to garden.

So on the last day of school field day, Laurie and Ms. Small organized a garden bonanza as a station for field day. The kids became workers, the two teachers bosses, and I manager. We hoed and planted, and weeded, and watered like mad, filtering the kids through the various tasks and out to other activities. All things said and done, we had planted sunflowers, flowers, pumpkins, corn, popcorn, tomatoes, lettuce, squash—it was a fucking great day.

26 Aug 2002

Walking through the doors after the summer break was Linda, pushing her baby cousin in a stroller. Now a fifth grader, she looked like a grown woman; I had nearly forgotten her name. Laurie came rushing from somewhere "Ooohh, look at you two, so tired!" She motioned us to follow her further into the school. We saw Ms. Small, she smiled at me and beamed at Sara who will also be working at the school; they chatted and I looked around, feeling more like a kid than an adult. Laurie, Sara, and I wandered out to the garden behind the school. Laurie and I had kept it alive during the summer, whole days of watering and weeding and all this food exploded out: corn, squash, lettuce, potatoes, tomatoes, herbs, strawberries, a watermelon or two, popcorn, sunflowers—and I think I'm forgetting some, but I'll tell you this. Each one is a story, events, moments: you know, each thing said and mumbled and written and sang and drawn and spoken by the kids. These weren't farming kids, these were inner-city kids, suburban kids; some gardened for *food*, some never gardened at all, and I fitted in the latter, but things change. So we found a few kids and began to harvest the corn. As more kids arrived at the school, so came awestruck parents, a tinge of pride forced a smile on my face, and the little ones came in waves. I hope the parents carry the awe home and wonder about their backyards and vacant lots, staring at empty cabinets and hungry mouths, wondering, "why not, why do I depend on 7-Eleven or ShopRite, or . . . "

A small Hispanic boy came rushing out of the gym doors, with intent in his eyes, stopped in front of the garden (intent gone?), looked around wild-eyed, exclaimed "WHAT HAPPENED?!" then disappeared into the corn to harvest, assisted by Sara and Laurie. Some kids' parents were milling about this unorganized thing and seemed to be watching from a distance; I wondered how to get them involved. Their faces shone with surprise and confusion. I didn't know what to make of it, how to describe it, or how to qualify it. The basket we set out was already full of corn, and almost every child who came out stopped in and asked, "can I help?" then picked a few ears and asked, "can I take it home?" Some kids showed their parents, others just asked.

I walked into the school to get some water, but was pulled out by Kara and Will, a problem child. It was easy to imagine him: black, poor, wide and dancing brown eyes. We walked into the corn stalks and disappeared. It was great being in the corn on those puffy-cloud days.

Over the summer, vandals had broken some windows on the outside of the school and smashed almost every watermelon and pumpkin. A few of the teachers and Laurie salvaged a part of a pumpkin, but it was accidentally thrown away by the new janitor. Some of the teachers used the corn the kids harvested as a first-day counting activity. After a summer of work in that garden, to have the kids' favorite fruits of my labor smashed hurt like a personal offense.

We never found out who attacked the garden, but we had a theory: Within a mile from the school is a trailer park, a particularly poor one. Some of the kids who go to Jonesville School live there. They are poor, on the last breath of home ownership. The trailers are jammed together, and the outside living space is tiny. The families who live there spend their days laboring for what they can never have, and their children wait. The kids idle away in front of televisions, waiting for their parents' attention. But their parents are too tired. When the kids are too old to listen, they find friends who can't wait any longer. There's a gas station nearby, a few businesses down the road, and a nearly vacant strip mall across the street. There is nothing around; if you live there you live at the junction of two roads and a highway, nothing more. Then of course there's the school down the street. That's the government, the city, an open evil sitting there as you wait for dreams that can never come to fruition because you can't afford them. In a culture of things, and in the wanting of things, to not have the ability to acquire them is to not have the ability to live (fully). This breeds dissidence. So the dissidence of these teenagers is funneled into hatred of the state, the rich, the things that seem so immediately at the root of their inability to acquire things.

We drove home on highways that span in every direction across farmland that soon will become small-town strip malls and private golf courses.

28 Aug 2002 garbage liberation analysis, fiesta, and after party

or

the secret to it all: you gotta eat lunch with the kids

Terry thought that this would be the right time to tell us about a recent experience with the dentist. Terry was talking about his silver teeth (of which he claimed to have almost all of them filled in). He described the dentist as being furious, annoyed at his mother for feeding him the way she does. Terry said that the dentist told him he had "a bad mother."

"Why?" I asked, notebook out, pen ready.

"I don't know." He said.

"Do you think it's what you eat?" I asked. He shrugged. Normally he talks my ear off, but today he just finished eating and disappeared. Something is awry.

After Terry left, Ariel leaned in toward me and smiled at Andy to be sure he was paying attention, then whispered, "Me and Andy brush our teeth at the same time, and Andy wants to be my boyfriend," Andy smiled. They finished eating, and Ariel grabbed me by the hand and dragged me outside. Boom, you open those doors from the gym, and I don't care if it's overcast, that fusion ball in the sky shocks your eyes because the gym is so poorly lit. Outside we found a bunch of kids running around, looking at things in the garden, pointing, screaming, jumping: "Can we pick the watermelon?" "Can I take this home?" "Can we pick the watermelon?" "What's that?" "What's that?" They kept hiding in the corn stalks (it was a puffy-cloud day, kids always hide in the corn on puffy-cloud days).

Everything was hectic. I let go of Ariel's hand and tried to get my bearings (what to do today?), and this girl Rachel holding a softball-size tomato ran up to me, "Look at my sweetheart!" she exclaimed. She raised high her heart, smiling, and a girl I call Bellissima (Bellissima means pretty face or wonderful or something like that in Italian, I hope) ran up with something on her mind. But whatever it was I missed it because she accidentally punched me in the crotch—ah, the pain of being tall in an elementary school.

Kids were swarming in the garden yelling at the grasshoppers, eating cherry tomatoes, "Can I pick this?" "Do we have potatoes?" "My teacher said I can stay after the bell!" "You're tall! Are you six feet tall?" "Where are the peppers?" "Are you in high school?" "Can I take this home?" "Is there a mouse here?" "Do we have strawberries?" "I heard there's a mouse here"; and Rachel holding up her tomato, stretching it toward sun and moon,

up
child,
higher,
heaven is in your hands . . .

An aide blew a whistle, the others followed suit, the children formed lines in tune with the yelling aides, and everyone disappeared into the building. I had accomplished nothing of what Laurie had asked, just answered kids questions and got punched in the balls; but it was only the third day of school, so there'd be time.

I've found that for some activities in the garden that once you explain to the kids what the goal is (provided there are enough competent adults and the kids are above first grade), sometimes they'll get into the work and almost get lost in it. Time will fly and you'll find yourself talking to a child messenger sent by a confused or angry teacher asking where her students are. Some teachers just leave you out there all afternoon (I think this is on purpose). Toward the end of the day, we got into one of those situations. I was digging for weeds with Natale and answering questions about my life. We had been talking about college when she asked if I lived with my parents.

"No, I live in a big house I co-own with a bunch of other students of my age, it's called a co-op."

"Oh."

"What about for holidays? What do you do on Christmas, do you see your parents?" I wasn't sure what to say here. Truth never hurts.

"I'm Jewish, I don't celebrate Christmas."

"Oh." Natale looked at Sara's back, then down, and decided to say, "Me too!" She smiled at the ground and started digging with more veracity. I laughed to myself noting the comment for later, though I thought it best to change the subject, but Natale cut off my thought.

"Yoooou like Sarraaaa." She whispered. I definitely had to change the subject.

"Do you garden at home?" I said, she giggled, she knew why I asked that.

"Yeah, I help my mom grow emergency food." She said nonchalantly still smiling.

"Natale, what's emergency food?" I asked, suddenly very attentive.

"It's food for when my mom's late on bills. Sometimes they shut off the water so my mom keeps it in big barrels, then we can drink when the water's off."

"Oh. That must not be fun," I sputtered.

We pulled weeds in silence until a kid came from her classroom and asked why everyone hadn't come back yet.

9 Sep 2002 bee dance

Lunch today:　Ham & cheese sandwich, goldfish crackers, peaches, tatertots.

Eating with Shari, a fifth-grade "future" cheerleader (according to her), told me that she saw kids stealing tomatoes from the garden at recess. Apparently they went to the office and asked if they could take them home, after being caught.

"How do you know all that Shari?"

"I don't know . . . Stop!" A boy across from her was sticking out his tongue, speckled ham, cheese, and something green in front of wide smile. "Boys are so gross!" She looked over at me, seemed to realize that I'm a boy, and sighed.

That afternoon a new teacher, Mrs. M, had asked for her class to come out and harvest tomatoes. Sara and I took them in tens; she turned the compost and I harvested the tomatoes for fifteen minutes at a time. Afterward, the kids just milled about, talking in little circles, hiding away from the three adults. They were calm and chatty ghetto children exploring: "What's that?" "Can I take it home?" After a minute, Mrs. M gathered them, a few faces stuffed with tomatoes. Then a boy found a small bee's nest. He started to chase a bee, wildly running, until the bee turned around; all of a sudden, the boy wanted to go in rather badly.

11 Sep 2002 orange alert

Lunch today: Corn dogs, tater tots, blueberry "loaves," "summer" peaches
　or
tuna and peanut butter bites and some other thing
Keep in mind,
there is as much
packaging,
as there is
food.

An absolutely beautiful day. My list for the day: pull up the watermelon patch, water the peppers, the strawberries, dig weeds near the lettuce, plant some lettuce.

Tiffany, a third or fourth grader told me that the kids weren't allowed outside because "they" were afraid of bombings. Apparently, the school board had decided that Lewiston schools, on September 11, 2002, were at threat of terrorist attacks because so many parents had called in with concerns. So I watered alone outside. After the first lunch, the door opened a peek, then shut quickly. I heard the sound of loud reprimanding from an adult to a child. Bored and for the hell of it, I knocked on the door. A kid said in a singsongy voice, "Nobody's home, even though you hear thousands of voices!"

After lunch a few teachers brought their kids out as Sara arrived. You can always count on the teachers to do the right thing, it seems that the administration had asked that no *recess* take place. The teacher that had wanted to work in the garden that day came to us and gave us her first batch of ten kids to plant lettuce. With no directions from Sara and me (except for where the seeds should go), they organized themselves and went about the task set before them, it was wonderful. The kids planted the lettuce with no help from me and Sara, really, we just watched the clouds. Most of the time the kids need all kinds of assistance to make sure everyone gets a turn, but today they just planted away.

The second batch of kids (about seven) had no interest in doing work, they wanted to throw tomatoes, to talk, yell. I got seven shovels and handed them to six kids at random and lined them up, I started singing some old work song. Two boys, Tyrone and Jacob started working with Sara. They were a little displeased about not digging (kids seem to really like digging holes), and kept saying "no, girl" to Sara's requests. She became a little displeased.

"You do not speak to me that way, you do not speak to *any* woman that way. That is not acceptable."

"Okay, girl," Jacob said.

"Sara is fine. Girl is not." Sara looked at Jacob, her face blank. He squirmed under her glare, and looked to Tyrone.

"Okay, girl," Tyrone glared at her. She looked at him in the same way, then at me. *We're wasting time.* I thought.

"You children want to dig?" I said, referring to Tyrone and Jacob purposely saying children.

"Yeah!" They yelled in unison, uncaring about my choice of words.

"Does anyone want to collect tomatoes with Sara?" I said. All the girls raised their hands. Off went most of the diggers, the two boys started digging with the rest. We had a little chat about talking to girls.

The third group was calm, though one little girl, Dani, started to cry the second she got outside. Her mother had said not to dirty her new shoes, but she really wanted to garden. I thought for a moment, all the other kids were quiet.

"Can everyone out here keep a secret?" I asked. When they mumbled back uncomfortable positive responses, I took off my shoes and socks.

"If you really want to work in the garden, and keep you shoes clean, then don't wear them! How's that?" She kept crying. Another girl looked over at Dani and said, "She cries at *everything,*" which made Dani cry more. "That was mean!" Sara said and looked unhappily at the speaker. Dani didn't know what to do, so I smiled at her and walked into the garden. She sputtered a moment more than sat down and took off her shoes and socks. The other kids started asking to do the same. I realized I'd be in the principal's office for this.

When that last group was to go in, one boy, Tom, stayed. I'd known Tom from Mrs. C's class last year; inside he was a problem child, but out here he was a master gardener.

Sara and I just kept working, saying good-bye to the kids leaving and talking with Tom. A few moments passed and one of us realized (probably Sara) that Tom wasn't supposed to be there. He sensed it and started pleading not to send him back "to her." Of course we said no, that it was time to go in, the normal gobbledygook you tell a kid in trouble. He put on a sad face and looked at me, then Sara. "That's not going to work, buddy, in," she said in response to his face, and added, "but we'll see you later, okay?" He smiled and started walking toward a different entrance than the one the other kids left through.

"Tom, go back to your class." I said sternly.

"I am!"

"Then go in the right door," I said.

"I am!"

Suddenly the door he was walking toward opened and a very annoyed old woman popped her head out and looked at Tom. "Where have you been?!" She said.

"I've been with Daniel!" He said.

"Who?" He pointed at Sara and me.

"We're part of the school's team of gardeners, for the soup night." I yelled over.

"Oh. Thank you for watching him." I remembered who she was right then, the substitute for Mrs. G. Tom must have left her classroom and came out as we were switching groups, smart fucker. As the door closed, we heard her say, "And where are your shoes?"

I'm *definitely* going to the principal's office for this.

2 Oct 2002 it's never going to be as bad as you think

really

Lunch today: Pancakes, sausage, pineapple, apple or grape juice
(whichever you ended up with).

Natale, Terry, and a few others came to sit with me. I didn't do a very good job with "crowding," today. If I sit after all the kids are seated then they don't crowd me. Terry, who rarely was at a loss for words, launched into his normal cascade. "Where do grapes come from?" and "Aren't raisins grapes? Because I heard . . . "

When Sara came in today, she told me we were to cook garden stuff for the soup night with two classes, Ms. Small's and Mrs. W's, but we needed more potatoes. So the second great dinosaur dig commenced, which resulted in more spuds than bones (though we did find some questionable rocks).

In the gym, a few lunch tables set in an L-shape were waiting to be staffed by kids. At the end farthest from the door were two Crock-Pots. There was an assortment of knives and some cutting boards. Next to those were some dirt-free onions and potatoes. Near the other table along the wall was a huge bin full of water. Another table had some herbs on it. This was all being set up while I was outside with some kids digging for more potatoes. Laurie and Ms. Small were telling the kids what they would be doing as Sara and I stood listening. Laurie would help collect more herbs, Sara would help wash potatoes, onions, carrots, and the like, while I would help cut all of it. Ms. Small and Mrs. W would preside over the whole affair.

From everyone else's point of view, it all went flawlessly; but for me and my fellow onion cutters, it was a right dreary day. We all sat there bawling; I reminded everyone not to touch their eyes, and of course they did; and to cut slowly, which most of them did. A few cut themselves and I took them to the office where the secretary would administer a bandage.

14 Oct 2002 you ask, where's Ricky?

Lunch today:

Hamburger	Hamburger	Hamburger
Pineapple juice	Pineapple juice	Pineapple juice
Peaches	Peaches	Peaches
Milk	Milk	Milk

The burgers were kind of white, perhaps from high fat content or low grade, or even high grade, I don't know, but I shoveled mine in like the rest of the kids. At first recess, I had only four kids. It was time to put the garden to "bed." Pull weeds, collect hay to be composted, pull out certain plants. After giving the kids their activities, Mark started up.

"Women sit around and do laundry while men do all the work." He said out of nowhere.

And Antone backed him up, "Yeah, but men watch football, women don't like football."

"And girls have cooties!" Mark yelled, playing his ace.

The girls spoke for themselves. Talking about how untrue that was, how their moms do work, and so on. The conversation soon turned to exclamations of cooties and who had (it? them?) and who liked whom. Eventually, I had them collect all the hay into a pile and jump on it, then jump in it. I love my job.

I don't remember when, but I had found out that Ricky would be moving to a different school. Ricky disappeared into the world, like Timmy's family before him, following the path of the transient poor around the world. You have to afford consistency.

21 Nov 2002 Soup From Our Stoop

Every student, the principal, the janitor, the teachers, the kitchen staff, the lunch aides participated to make what happened on November 21 possible. And those who came had a fucking great time.

The school staff, the student helpers, and the university volunteers arrived early. It was snowing pretty hard, but we expected a good turnout. Laurie had an advertising team who made flyers and a radio announcement or two. At first, we just kind of played around, set everything up, and hugged one another, and we, the university students, received our congratulations and thanks from the teachers. I rigged up the school's announcement system to play Dave Brubeck's "Time Out," after doing some "helloooo Jonesville, this is the Garden Guy, Daniel, here to welcome you to this year's Soup From Our Stoop—first annual we hope!" kind of stuff like the SUNDAY, SUNDAY, SUNDAY! announcements for monster truck rallies.

If you were to walk into the school, you'd be greeted by two sets of kids, the first was at the entrance to the gym. They'd show you where the sign-in book was, then explain that you could either buy a Styrofoam bowl and soup for five dollars, or a kid-made bowl and soup for ten dollars. The next set would help you choose a kid-made bowl and or show you where the soup was. The school purchased some nice linen to put the bowls on and candles. The lights were low and there was an old set of pictures showcasing the garden. Then I helped the lunch aide set up some bread donated by a local bakery, and Laurie ran around schmoozing and introducing people. I guess. I ran around getting things from places and cleaning up messes. As everything was toning down, the kid who doesn't eat human food came out of nowhere and gave me a cup of coffee, great kid.

It went perfectly; we raised two thousand dollars for the Greater Lewiston Food Bank, and the Jonesville School garden. There was a huge turnout, some of the kids were interviewed by Zoom, a PBS kid's show, and the local news showed up.

When it was over, we took turns mopping the gym so the janitor didn't have to—she just stood there laughing and yelling out orders. Sara, Kristan, and I were the last to leave (save the janitor). It had started snowing, one of those warm snows. We drove back laughing and recounting kids' comments.

2 Sep 2003 ¿principal nueva?

I walked in late and Mike was directing some kids with tomato picking. I started to assist, when their teacher called them to come inside. A boy with a strange dumbfounded smile looked around. "This is a cute garden!" he says, then runs off. We laughed. Mike nods toward the kid, "that's Joshua," he says. As the second lunch kicked in, Mike left for class and I made the mistake of allowing too many kids into the garden. The kids went a little nuts, harvesting things that weren't ready. Defiantly harvesting a shitload of tomatoes, they went nuts, filled a huge box and a garbage bag of tomatoes. Well the job is done, not in an organized manner but it's done.

Second lunch filled its quota and the kids left. I cleaned up, talked with the new janitor for a moment, and asked Mrs. F how I should institute a system like last year's; she directs me to the new principal. I liked the old "new" principal from last year. She was easy to work with and supported everything we did. With Mike and I just out at the school this year, we needed all the help we could get. Her office is full of papers; she dressed like a business woman, very nicely. I sit down, introduce myself, and shot right into it. "Last year we had a system wherein the teachers would select the time and what they wanted to do in the garden. We just made sure that it went well, and made possible our common goal, the soup night." My little rant went on for a moment, talking about the soup night, the great lunch system we had last school year, and I stopped. I was like those guys who stop you in the street to try to sell you Jesus in twenty seconds or less ("Hi, blah blah blah blah blah Jesus!!).

"Well, Daniel, this year is going to be different," she began. "You see, we have certain benchmarks and standards (*What is this jargon? Must hold attention! I'll just write it down, that'll make it look like I'm paying attention, then look over it later!*) that we have to meet in the district, and I would like you to tie those in with the garden. In other words, Daniel, you need to approach the garden with the state benchmarks and standards in mind. You need to be more directed, you need to work conscientiously with the classroom. Ask yourself, 'For what purpose am going to plant tomatoes?' or 'How does planting tomatoes fit in the curriculum?' Do you understand?"

"What are benchmarks and standards?" I asked.

"They are kind of like a set of guidelines each teacher must meet for their class." This went on awhile, my notes were growing more and more sparse, until three phrases took up the rest of the page. "Instructional time," "prior planning," "documentation." I don't know what they meant, but of course guesses can be made. I looked over at the clock and decided it's time to go, we said our good-byes, and I left. The school secretary laughed as I walked past her desk.

"See ya later, Danny," she says.

I drove to Mike's, he was outside. "Hey man, I just talked to the new principal. She seems nice. Supports the garden," I yelled over.

"Good," Mike answered.

"No more planning in the doorway though."

11 Sep 2003 retired pro

Last year, on September 11, the fear of the parent-teacher organization, or the genius of Lewiston schools' superintendent, or some other authority who rose to the level of their incompetence, didn't allow kids on the playground for fear of a terrorist attack. The then principal and I had a good laugh about it. This year, nothing happened, no one stupid did anything stupid, and the doors stayed open, the kids ran out and the people rejoiced. I found Mike at the grow cart. We had agreed to clean it for Ms. Small.

We chatted about the post-lunch-recess problem and decided that I'll just have the kids line up to enter the garden and be stringent about it: only a few in at a time. We finished up and reported back to Ms. Small who was in the process of taking her class outside for a break. The class flies out, Mike and I make a beeline to the garden only to find it already occupied by a few kids wandering around. One kid with a blond mullet is looking up at the sunflowers. I walk over to him.

"I like sunflowers. I tried to make one at home but it died." He looks at me.

"Did you water it?" I ask.

"Yeah. It probably didn't get enough sun." He looks at the ground.

"Maybe. You'll try again right?" I looked down at him and smiled.

"I guess." He walked off without looking up.

A few minutes later, Chris (the kid who used to punch us in the balls our first year), Joshua, the mullet kid, Mike, and I were weeding. Joshua wasn't really weeding as much as walking around, looking at things. "I like playing in the bushes," he says, then runs off. A pair of grasshoppers jumped out of nowhere, one is sitting on the other. The kids go nuts, "Why are they riding each other?!" Mike and I exchanged a glance: shit, the birds and the bees.

"They're um, mating." I say. That's it, the kids don't respond. No questions of what "mating" is. Sweet. The kids just started weeding again after a minute or two.

After a few more minutes the mullet kid asked if he can go swing.

"Sure, you're here by choice my man, we've got no hold over you, she does though." Mike pointed at his teacher, and he runs off. The rest of us keep weeding away until I noticed Chris staring at the swings like they're his recently lost love.

"Chris, it's okay, no hard feelings if you want to swing," I say.

"I used to be a swinger," he responds, still sad looking.

"What, you mean professionally?" I say.

"Yeah . . . "

Mike stifles a laugh. "What happened?"

"I lost my style," he says. We laughed as Chris smiled.

16 Sep 2003 the problem of the mating grasshoppers

We're picking tomatoes (what's left of them), and two grasshoppers jump out one on top of the other again, no one notices for a minute. Then a little kid yells, "Woh, they're sleeping! One is sleeping on the other!"

Another, older kid, retorts all singsongy, "no they're maaating."

"Ohhh . . . ," the first says.

Two more jumped out, "damn they're having a good season" I think to myself.

"Two more mating!" A third kid, Zack, yells.

Luckily the aides started to whistle just as my mouth opened to try to form some kind of explanation that wouldn't land me in court or something.

"Okay, gardeners, time to go in!" I say.

"See ya later, school's whistling!" Mike says to his own chuckle.

"Hey look!" Joshua yells as he stands to leave, "all the flowers are tired!"

"No, they're just getting too heavy to hold themselves up. It's okay," Mike said while using his huge hands to illustrate. Josh just smiles and runs off. On my way out, a teacher told me that one of her students had been caught with a four-inch blade on the bus. He was always great help in the garden, I didn't want to believe it.

this is important

Me: "Do you like gardening?"

Marque: "I watch gardening on TV . . . this is good."

Field day is always the best day of the year, it's an extravaganza, it's as close to absolute freedom as most people will ever have. Some families show up and there'll be babies tottering around and older siblings hanging out, it's great. There's tons of teacher-run activities to choose from, and the kids love it. A bunch of people worked in the garden, and I rototilled the soon-to-be greenhouse ground. I had three helpers clearing away rocks and string and making up plant names. One of them brought along his father who asked to rototill, I gave it up and he found something in that smelly loud thing.

The whole time he used it, he had the look of a man rediscovering something absolutely wonderful, he looked as if he was about to cry, or laugh, or, maybe

something greater
a secret   from

            his   past.

CHAPTER EIGHT

A methodology of letting go, getting lost, and finding my way.

What we observe is not nature herself,
but nature exposed to our method of questioning.
—Werner Heisenberg, *Physics and Philosophy*

My method of questioning circles around an ever-changing, elusive, now-you-see-it-now-you-don't phenomenon in a very uncertain world. The right questions today may be the wrong questions tomorrow. Sure, go ahead and prepare your research design. Plan away. But my advice, don't hold on too tight. Constructivist/phenomenological methodologies require a certain spaciousness of thinking that allows for things to emerge on their own terms. Oh sure, we can review the literature and find those who have tromped this ground before us and conclude that things will go this way or that. Theories abound. Conclusions, too. Hitch your wagon. But in the end, let the kids or the teachers or the spawning salmon or whatever your "subject" have their way with you; be present to their every word and wiggle. Pay attention. Resist that pressing urge to make sense of it all, to impose your questions, categories, and order too soon.

letting go (research design).

The methodology I employed in this study was an extension of my world-view. Guba and Lincoln (1998) state that ontology, epistemology, and methodology are logically interconnected in such a way that to address one constrains how the others must be addressed. Or, quite simply, how best to get at the data and stay true to yourself and others? I would be "divided no more" (to steal a phrase from Parker Palmer). This time around, my research would be an outgrowth of my relational worldview. I had abdicated the legitimization of conventional science for a way of knowing that honored this intricate web of relationships I call home. I could no longer participate in the "objective," numerate, monolithic way of doing science that has stripped my beloved agriculture of her beauty. And so this was a strategic move into the less-comfortable qualitative spaces of tangled subjectivities, participatory methods, messy texts, and conflicting interpretations. As agriculturists, we have chosen a vocation of living things; why then is our research so lifeless. Seems I am surrounded by an ideological obsession with statistical knowledge. John Rowan says, "There is too much measurement going on . . . Orthodox research produces results which are statistically significant but *humanly insignificant*" (1981, xiv, italics added). In the agricultural disciplines, we are producing knowledge that includes the "other," but I ask you, where are they? Reading through our journals of scholarship, I find statistical representations of the other, but rarely do we allow our research "subjects" to speak. Apparently our subjects are nameless, faceless, emotionless beings: not a very interesting lot to study one would imagine. Little wonder our rural communities are dissolving; we have written them out of existence.

What began as a typical qualitative research design—purposive sample, interview protocol, content analysis, and case study write-up—quickly evolved into an emergent, participatory, and performative learning community. My first taste of "letting go" occurred when I attempted to introduce the teachers to the garden curriculum I wanted them to pilot for my study. Authored at a university a thousand miles away, this curriculum was thoroughly researched, beautifully packaged, and I was offering it for free. What's not to love? Much to my dismay, I could not find one teacher willing to pilot this curriculum in her classroom; they politely said no thank you. As described in chapter one, curricular change is constant in this school district. These teachers did not want or need another new curriculum. After observing curricular change for over four years now, my new mantra is, curriculum is a four-letter word. Teachers are subjected not only to constant curricular change from their district and the state, but every educational snake oil salesman, commodity group, or school reformist who walks in the door has a magic-bullet curriculum to peddle. I might add that the Elevator Escalator Safety Foundation has a very attractive curriculum shelved among the scores of other curricula at Jonesville School. The garden curriculum that I was proposing was soon to be added among these files. It was at that point in time, I began to seriously doubt the wisdom of my research design; the plans I had so carefully laid out in my proposal no longer made sense. Time to let go and listen.

Paraphrasing Parker Palmer (1983), the goal of this type of knowing is a reunification, reconstruction, and re-creation of broken selves and broken worlds. In other words, our epistemologies hold the potential to heal or make whole again what modernity tore apart. We are in a reciprocal relationship with what we have come to know; the positivistic goal of objectivity—the origins of our broken ontology—is no longer held up as an ideal. I have come to recognize that a dynamic participative reality can only be discovered with participative methods; in other words, knowledge is co-created not just in our classrooms but also at our research sites. The socially constructed nature of reality dictates that reality be elicited and understood in communion with "the other." My research proposal that had been written a thousand miles away, a priori, without setting foot in the school (mind you this was a requirement of both the school district and my university institutional research review board) was grossly out of touch with the realities of the lived experience of the students and teachers. What became obvious was the need to dissolve traditional boundaries between investigator and investigated, forming instead a community of inquiry. This community would share the responsibility for research design and surfacing the most pressing questions and issues. What became of greatest import was the consensual construction of an appropriate situated methodology.

My second experience with letting go occurred as I began to interview the teachers. During the course of these interviews, my predetermined interview protocol felt stiff and lifeless. The protocol was semi-structured and I granted a wide berth, allowing conversations to take unexpected twists and turns; however, something was missing. The interviews I conducted felt artificial, never quite capturing the *lived experience* of the teachers. Time and time again I would leave the interview feeling disappointed in the process and the data I had collected. Further, asking teachers to set aside time for an interview always felt like an imposition; their days were overscheduled as it was. I could ask for a story but I never got it. Jerome Bruner (1991) reminds us that narrative is not only representative of reality but also *constitutive* of reality, and there's the rub. Over the course of this study, I have found that stories are not low-hanging fruit simply to be plucked during an interview—it is not just a matter of *asking for* stories or *listening to* stories but rather of learning to *be with* stories. Stories unfold in relationship over time, both rare commodities these days. This is one of the most precious gifts I take away from this study, that the good stuff, the really good stuff, the blow-your-hair-back data, comes in the form of the stories we tell one another, if you are lucky enough to forge those bonds. So stay awhile. Hang around. Go drink a few beers with the teachers on a Friday afternoon. Do it again, and again. Scrap the interview. The world is brimming with stories if only we will stay put and pay attention.

Finally, I'd like to mention that this letting go of the research design made a clearing for all to become more intimately involved with the project. What once was going to be *their* task (teachers gardening with their students) became *our* project. What once was going to unfold in a linear fashion—project implementation, observation, interview, analysis, and write-up—became a much more iterative and fluid process. Further, I could no longer stand back and observe as the dispassionate researcher, nor could the teachers resist involvement in the curricular design. We're women—we connect, we embrace, we draw near. For me this was the moment when I made an ideological shift from a "qualitative researcher" to a "participatory researcher." Prior to this, the latter was something I had read about in books but had no notion of what it actually meant. Fieldnotes became retrospective fieldnotes—the choice between notepad and pencil or shovel and seeds was quite clear. Interviews were replaced with heartfelt hallway conversations transcribed after the fact, all points of departure in my journey of letting go.

Having learned to let go, I began to see that the design of this study could quite comfortably reside under the umbrella of an indeterminate ontology or emergent design (Lincoln and Guba 1985). As phenomenologists, we accept uncertainty about our research design in this highly uncertain world. Uncertainty ultimately turns to our advantage; it frees us from the intellectual myopia of hyperdetermined research projects (Richardson 1997). Emergent research design was congruent with my understanding of a participatory cosmos. The path to this way of knowing is not clearly marked, nor should it be. Peter Kahn describes the constructivist path this way:

> We have a choice, to follow the trails or not. Here is what happens to me when I choose the trails. I cover lots of ground fast. I start thinking about past experiences and future possibilities, and as my mind chatters to itself time goes by and miles are covered. In con-

trast, when I move off trail my mind becomes more alert. My perceptions become keener. Each moment I have decisions to make. I pay more attention to the landscape. It is a wonder, a pleasure. It is also unsettling; I take the risk of getting lost. With similar alertness and feelings in seeking to understand the human relationship with nature we move off trail into uncharted territory. Questions help set our course. (1999, 51)

In fact, emergent design is described as axiomatic to naturalistic inquiry, for, as Lincoln and Guba state, "It is inconceivable that enough could be known ahead of time about the many realities to devise the design adequately" (1985, 41). This uncertainty, this ambiguity of design, may be perceived as a weakness by conventional science; however, it is precisely this uncertainty that I have found to be indispensable in understanding the lived experience of others. For in our receptivity to the emergent nature of phenomena, we acknowledge a participatory cosmology. Our research design becomes nimble, adaptable, and exquisitely finessed to the local context of the study and the unfolding complexity of the universe.

data collection.

Purposive sampling (Patton 1990) was used to locate participants willing to converse about their experiences with the garden and garden-based curriculum. The power of purposive sampling is situated in its ability to ground the inquiry in emic views of local respondents. This project focused on a sample of five key informant teachers, approximately forty students, the school principal, and support staff from Jonesville School. This type of sampling deviates from probability sampling with its final aim of generalizability to a larger population. Rather, the logic in purposive sampling lies in selecting information-rich respondents for study. A purposive sample shifts the emphasis from quantity to quality, from breadth to depth. Aggregate data stripped of time and place were not a goal of this study. For, as we have seen time and time again in the social sciences, "the trouble with generalizations is that they don't apply to particulars" (Lincoln and Guba 1985, 110).

The teachers and students who emerged as participants in the telling of this story were not a fixed number—a static slide, no. Observing the ebb and flow of research participants provides useful insights into the challenges of qualitative research in our public schools. Why do certain children and teachers stay with the process long enough to construct their "stories" while others drop out of the study? The revolving door of poverty coupled with high teacher and staff attrition is a continued challenge in this work. As I write this section I can count on one hand the number of research participants who remain at the school. Purposive sampling allowed for the flexibility to actively seek out participants who remained connected to this study.

Ruth Behar (1996, 5) suggests that what we do in ethnography is a form of "witnessing." When thinking about the data collection in this study, witnessing seems to fit. There was no "instrument" used in this study—no paper-and-pencil survey—instead, my commitment was to heart-wide-open witnessing. Data collection was initially carried out using traditional qualitative methods, including interview, observation, and document analysis. These methods were originally selected because of their likely fit to the study; however, other more appropriate and informative methods emerged during the course of the study. The overriding issue here was how might I best access, understand, or otherwise comprehend the phenomena of inquiry.

A demonstration of the necessity for a more participatory methodology came during my first month on site. At this time, I was offered an invitation from several teachers to attend their last faculty meeting of the school year. During the course of the meeting, the topic of pending district-wide curricular changes was addressed. The building's district curriculum advisor spoke up and made a plea for input from the Jonesville School teachers regarding their views on the curriculum. A long and pregnant pause settled on the meeting. Again, the advisor made a plea for input, this time followed by a comment that the district had solicited this information once already by paper survey and the response rate had been a dismal twenty surveys returned out of a mailing of 1,600. This comment broke the silence and the floodgates opened. Teachers voiced concerns regarding a lack of trust, lack of time, and lack of freedom to express what they really wanted to say. These women were calling out to be genuinely heard, to tell their story, and not to be treated as a number. One particularly articulate teacher cried out, "They expect us to teach to the whole student but they don't model that behavior when dealing with us!" What I heard was that these teachers wanted to fully participate in knowledge construction. What a mistake it would be for me to simply attempt "data collection" without including the teachers in the design of the study. Here again was a moment of letting go: the data I had gathered in my interviews paled by comparison to what I had learned by simply witnessing the lived experience of these teachers.

Thomas Schwandt (1999) suggests that, sustaining the conditions for open dialogue is necessary for hermeneutical understanding. In dialogue, a group has access to a larger pool of common meaning that cannot be obtained on an individual basis (Bohm 1996). Central to this process must be a commitment to create a "space" characterized by generative listening, suspension of assumptions, and, paradoxically, intention without direction. Genuine dialogue prevents one from being trapped in what David Bohm characterizes as the "theater of our own thoughts." I have found this to be true when following an interview protocol; all too often I walked away with only a mirroring-back of my own constructions and thoughts. Alternatively, when I let go and follow the conversation to where it takes us, I have discovered insights into my research that would normally not be revealed. Entering into the flow of dialogue allows for fuller participation and authorship from our respondents. Dialogue creates common ground for shared meaning and the healing of fragmented thought. Rather than trying to organize the parts into a meaningful whole, direct access to the whole is possible and is made explicate. This collective way of thinking is inherently more powerful than the individual thought, according to Bohm. He compares the power of collective thought to that of a laser, producing an intense beam of coherent light. In dialogue, our scattered thoughts are aligned into shared meaning. This bears striking similarities to the ideal of hermeneutical understanding that Thomas Schwandt (1999) describes. Citing Kenneth Gergen, Schwandt argues in favor of "understanding that is not contained within me, or within you, but in that which we generate together in our form of relatedness" (Gergen 1988, 47). This, then, is the ideal that draws me away from the to and fro of interview *technique* into the relational flow of our *lived conversations*.

In thinking about data collection, I have learned to attend to the stories. When hearing the truth of another's story, we actively participate in knowledge creation. This is a reciprocal knowing of the self and other in dynamic interplay—both intensely personal and social. This way of knowing requires that we are fully present with one another. Narration—the telling of our story—is one of the primary sense-making activities of the human experience (Bruner 1990; Polkinghorne 1988). In telling our story, we are able to sequence events into unified episodes; this develops into plot and, by being in plot, events take on significance and meaning (Polkinghorne 1991). There is a "temporal thickness" in the act of narration. A narrative concept of self incorporates both recollected past and anticipated future into a unified whole. The temporal order we find in the narrative is more than points in time; the ordering refers to recognizable boundaries of passage through "openings" and "closings" along the way (Mishler 1995). This connected succession or sequencing suggests a causal or thematic relation among events beyond temporal order. The "order of the telling" (Goodman 1980) can offer significant insights to qualitative researchers using narrative analysis. Any particular event gains its meaning within the configuration of the whole (Mattingly 1994). Much like music, when hearing narrative, we should listen for the contribution that each event makes to the unity of the arrangement. Further, with each retelling, there may be a reordering of events designed for the particular context and occasion of the telling.

In considering the use of narrative as a method for data collection in this study, I was particularly drawn to the literature on the "work" that stories do for the storyteller. Many theorists view our construction of narrative as primary to the development of the self. Narrative analysis from this perspective might elucidate the progression, stasis, or digression of the lives of our research participants as lived through a culturally available story. Arthur Frank (1995) develops a compelling typology based on this re-creation of the self through the narrative. Frank sees narrative purpose as twofold: first, stories "repair damage" that has been done to a person's sense of where they are in life and where they are going—they are a way of redrawing the maps and finding new destinations; and second, the need to tell our story is more immediate: we need to tell people what is happening now in our lives, often from conditions of strain, fatigue, pain, illness, uncertainty, or fear. These "interruptions" threaten our sense of temporality, in other words, a past that leads into a present that sets in place a foreseeable future.

According to Frank's typology, there are three general types of story lines that serve this function of reclaiming the self: the restitution narrative, the chaos narrative, and the quest narrative. In the restitution narrative one should listen for a pattern of misery-remedy-comfort. This age-old story line offers limited agency or responsibility to the teller. The remedy typically is provided not by the storyteller but from some outside source. In the chaos narrative, there is a complete absence of sequence or causality. This plot imagines life never getting better. There is a profound loss of control, and we hear a conscious giving up of the self. The third category Frank describes is the quest narrative. This story line follows Joseph Campbell's hero's journey closely. Unlike in the chaos narrative, in the quest narrative the teller is actively crafting his or her own story. The quest begins with a "call" or "departure" on the journey that occurs at the time of interruption. During the journey there are trials, but eventually the self gains some truth from the experience and returns bearing this truth founded in pain or suffering. Frank's quest narrative resonated deep within me. I feel as if I am returning from such a journey. Certainly this framework for narrative analysis has profoundly affected my understanding of an "interrupted life." The truths that I discovered during my quest journey following the loss of my father propelled this work forward. I could not help but carry this method for understanding lived experience into the field with me.

getting lost.

Patti Lather (2001) begins to theorize the concept of "getting lost" as a methodological stance. In thinking about postfoundational nonmastery ways of knowing, Lather advocates a more "tentative voice" and "stumbling practices" that force us to "stand open to the inconclusiveness" of the realities we represent. This new mark of rigor demands a refusal to deliver tidy, mastery narratives of linear progress, or what she calls "comfort" texts. I am drawn to this place of no easy answers and moments of despair as I find myself writing in "failure's intensity when history takes fire and meaning is swallowed up" (Blanchot 1986, 47). I wish I could write a happily-ever-after story—a "comfort text"—for these are children with basic needs going unmet. These are children with little or no access to fresh, nutritious food. Not to mention love and attention, literacy and health care, clean water, security and safety. It is a profusion of needs. Overwhelming, ever present. There is little comfort to be found. We are failing the most vulnerable in society in unspeakable ways every day. Unspeakable—yes. Dare I write about the failures I see among these teachers and families I hold so dear? Dare I write about a public school system so broken, so dysfunctional, yet at the same time willing to take a chance and let me in, allowing me to peer into their darkest places? How dare I? Dare I write about my own gaping failures? Days when I could have, should have, didn't care, selfish, opportunistic, shortcuts. Days when I am ready to chuck it all and walk away. One step forward, two steps back. It is all too easy to "get lost" in the world of public schooling in an urban school district. Teacher burnout has taken four of my closest research partners in the past year. I am lost without them. The flight and mobility associated with poverty regularly takes children from the study: one day they are with you and the next they are gone. Lost. We are on our fifth principal now in a matter of three years. One loss after another.

And so I deal with this excessive otherness that defies all analysis and representation with messy texts, polyvocality, poetry, and performance ethnography.

"It doesn't seem like research," a young graduate student innocently comments following a presentation of my work to a qualitative research methods class. My spine stiffens, stomach flips, don't look, there it is, my deepest fear out there in the open. Self-doubt tumbles in, *not* research? This nomenclature we hold so dear in the academy, out there flopping around on the table. The grad student continues, "It feels more like wisdom," her eyes well up with tears. "Your words remind me of my mother, who is the farthest thing from the academy." Hearing her explanation, I can breathe again. I reply with a question, "Is it possible that our research here in the academy can be something other than rational, objective headwork?"

Lost in the academy, I doubt an optimistic answer to this question. Though Lather's words afford me some solace:

> What all of this means is perhaps best evoked in Pitt and Britzman's concept of "difficult knowledge," knowledge that works otherwise than to secure and revise claims through data. Attempting to theorize the qualities of difficult knowledge, they distinguish between "lovely knowledge" and difficult knowledge. The former reinforces what we think we want from what we find and the latter is knowledge that induces breakdowns in representing experience. Here accepting loss becomes the very force of learning and what one loves when lovely knowledge is lost is the promise of thinking and doing otherwise, within and against Enlightenment categories of voice, identity, agency, and experience so troubled by incommensurability, historical trauma and the crisis of representation. (2001, 4)

And so what I love "when lovely knowledge is lost" are these malleable, organic, woman-full ways of doing the difficult work of research. I love the days of losing my mind and finding my heart totally immersed in the garden with the children. I love writing with the fourth graders on Friday mornings—their words are so fresh, so pure, offered straight up—which stands in stark contrast to my own highly politicized writing. I love the frenzy and cold, hard reality of teachers' lounge conversations; here is where I learned to do ethnography—to study culture. I love that doing difficult knowledge keeps me open to "lines of flight" (Deleuze and Guattari 1983). Lines of flight are about the pull and velocity of being carried away in another direction from our planned research trajectory. In my case, hungry children were one such "difficult" line of flight. The revolving door of poverty, teacher burnout, and the overwhelming force of mandated curriculum are other lines of flight that keep me lost yet are the force of learning.

finding my way.

I have learned to live with these losses, and in so doing I have found my way. In this "world on fire," the certainties I have discovered all coalesce around our ability to make lasting connections, form bonds, slow down, nurture reciprocity, and build trust. The data collection methods I eventually used all emerged from the ruins of a "lovely" research proposal that was not grounded in the realities and chaos of public schooling. The methods that now stand as my most trusted tools of the trade are participant observation coupled with retrospective fieldnotes and the persistent gathering of narratives, documents, and photographs. What follows is a more detailed description of my use of these methods.

Participant observation.

Participant observation is "split at the root," writes Behar (1996) It strikes me that this term carries with it the lineage of a divided and distanced science; not a heritage I am particularly proud of, yet nonetheless this is our family tree. This grammatical demarcation between subject and object doesn't settle well. How do we make way for a new social science, a new marriage in the family, one that reconciles this schism? Can we not go into our fields of study with our eyes, hands, *and* hearts wide open? Retrospective fieldnotes relieved me of the burden that "observation" suggests, that is, that I will somehow capture reality with my notepad and pen while in the field. I can honestly tell you that I tried to do this for several weeks and finally let it go; I just couldn't do it, just couldn't stand back and observe.

First, there is too much observation going on in our schools: field supervisors observing student teachers, principals observing teachers, teaching mentors observing students, teachers observing pupils, parents observing teachers. All this observation makes me itchy. Our schools really don't need one more body sitting around observing. Count me out. Second, there is just too much to do; 250 children all starved for attention, I have yet to find a day at school when my hands, heart, and eyes weren't fully engaged. It's too late for participant observation; I can't keep the distance. And that's okay by me, for as Behar so eloquently confesses, "anthropology that doesn't break your heart just isn't worth doing anymore." (1996, 177).

Retrospective fieldnotes.

It soon became quite clear that taking fieldnotes in the presence of that fierce heat of a curious child just wasn't tenable. The kids wrapped themselves around my heart and wouldn't let go. They demanded my all. Notes would have to come after the fact; the needs of the children were too great to ignore: Love me, feed me, show me, look at me, "Mrs. Thorp listen to what I wrote." "Laurie look at what I found!" "Can I go outside with you, too?" "Take me with you." "Pick me!" I soaked up all the participation this school had to offer and trusted that the observations would pour out onto the paper later each evening. Sure enough they did. This shift from fieldnotes to retrospective fieldnotes felt both liberating and transgressive. What would my committee think? Was this still research? But is it data? Will it count? Is it valid? At some point along the way two things happened: first, I "came clean" to my committee—"Yes, of course you must continue doing your study this way, and you must write about it. There is not enough written about the methods participatory researchers employ." At the same time, I came across a wonderful article by Jean Jackson entitled, "Déjà Entendu: The Liminal Qualities of Anthropological Fieldnotes." In reading Jackson's article, I took great comfort in her study of seventy anthropologists and their feelings toward their fieldnotes. I found I was not alone in experiencing a constant tension between doing fieldwork and writing fieldnotes. Respondents in Jackson's study echoed my frustration with the form (often incomplete, sketchy, cryptic) and the process (exhausting work taking hours to capture ten minutes of field experience) of doing fieldnotes. However challenging fieldnotes are, Jackson confirms that they mediate the conflicted existence of being both insider and outsider.

> Anthropology is a combination of this interaction with people and writing. Fieldnotes is an intermediate step between the immediate experience of interaction and the written document . . . no matter how much one may understand the other, it doesn't have a certain kind of reality until it's put into fieldnotes. (1990, 15)

I can say that Jackson's article allowed me to make peace with my fieldnotes, completely changing my relationship with the document and, by association, changing my relationship to the fieldwork. Eventually, I learned to stop self-censoring my notes and to grant myself the freedom of the page. I learned to make this a space of no judgment and that made all the difference.

Documents and artifacts.

Documentation (written or recorded material not prepared specifically in response to a request from the researcher) emerged as a natural source of data in this study. Lincoln and Guba (1985) detail the usefulness of documentation to include stability of information, contextual relevance, richness of information, and natural language of the setting, and finally, documents are nonreactive. The utilization of school artifacts and documents as data was not originally planned or proposed. However, student garden journals, garden maps, photographs, garden stories, poetry and artwork, notes from teachers, school newsletters, recipes, dog-eared seed catalogues, and clipped magazine articles, all began to accumulate—impossible to ignore. What ethnographic message did these artifacts hold? Read as a "text," what story is told by these documents? Further, I was drawn into the visual quality of these data: the colors, shapes, forms, and textures, all provided a depth of description I had learned was so necessary for good ethnographic work.

Peter Manning states concern regarding the logocentrism found in most ethnographic representation, wherein the weight of the argument is carried by and large by the written word of the author. The challenge of postmodern ethnography, he states, is to heighten our sensitivity to *other equally valid modes of representation*. Manning asks, "How is it the unsayable, the deep structure of human lives, is conveyed by such words, and how do words capture that which cannot be written?" (1995, 267). Douglas Harper (1987, 2000), in describing photo elicitation as an underutilized qualitative method, encourages us as sociologists to construct a "visual narrative." These visual images encourage readers to take a closer look at the small social worlds of our inquiry. Visual imagery adds a layer of complexity to our texts and representations pointing at specific moments of human interaction. They are, as Roland Barthes (1981) says, "moments of resurrection."

Photographs.

I have found that photographing the teachers and children during their participation in the project was one of the least obtrusive and most "natural" methods of data collection available to me. After sharing this observation with several teachers, we agreed that allowing the children to talk about the photos would generate narrative data for the study; it could also serve as an important literacy practice. On a regular basis, I sat with the children and allowed them to narrate the photographs for me. For most of the children, telling a story with temporal order was something quite new. The photographs of their previous activities in the garden were meaningful scaffolding to learn the art of narration—connecting the past, present, and future. Responses to the images of the children in the garden varied from flights of fancy to realist description. Some children used this time to suggest changes in the garden plans, while others used it as a time to relive special moments in the garden with a friend. As Douglas Harper (2000) states, this form of visual sociology integrates seeing into the research process. Capturing a photographic image is quick, information rich, nimble (I can throw it around my neck and still have two hands free for children or shovels), inexpensive, digital, and evocative. However, there were other more compelling considerations that supported my use of this method of data collection. I began to notice during my first few days on site that the children loved to have their picture taken. This symbolic ritual of affirmation is meaningful to them, and so I did it, again and again. Whether it was pride in what they had accomplished or simply joy in being noticed, either case was warrant enough. Lending further support, the children continuously hounded me if I failed to bring in copies of their pictures following my visit. Not only did the children request photographs so did the teachers. The teachers were using photographs for bulletin boards, class newsletters, open house posters, and writing activities. Other teachers had joined me in photographing the progress of the garden, and now it is not unusual for me to find reprints in my mailbox at school, little reminders of the validity of this method. Photographing, it seems, has become *a culturally acceptable method* of data collection at Jonesville School. I do it, the teachers do it, the children love it, it fills a need; what could be a better fit? Finally, there is a whisper of beauty in the photographs. Beautiful photos fulfill *my need* for this study to be a thing of beauty, and words somehow aren't enough. In fact, words have been too much in our world of research, overshadowing the truth that arises out of beauty. For how does language convey the beauty in the children's smiles as they anticipate their first crop of strawberries? It doesn't. Poets have tried, and they come pretty darn close, but I want you to *see* these beautiful, proud smiles and those delicate strawberry blossoms on that sun-filled afternoon in April.

Narrative.

Jerome Bruner (1991) asks, "How do we cobble stories together to make them into a whole of some sort?" Bruner suggests that a salient feature of

narrative in constructing and understanding human interaction is narrative accrual. Narratives do accrue, and at some point we eventually create a representation of a "culture" or a "tradition" or the like. The hundreds of little stories I collected as "data" did in fact accrue; they came together to tell a bigger story requiring very little work on my part. What I have observed is that through our mutual accountability or sense of community we weave our individual narratives into a meaningful whole. This larger narrative is what holds us together, or more troubling, the lack thereof is why we fall apart.

Narrative analysis may also point to the restrictive, or alternatively, liberating power of culturally sanctioned stories. We can view the work that the narrative does in the constant re-telling and ever-changing degree of agency afforded the narrator. Additionally, stories provide institutional functions: working to provide structure, transmit social truths, guide behavior, and maintain relationships. I found this type of narrative framework especially useful in understanding change (the introduction of the garden) in an institutional context (a public school district). At a different level of analysis, these unfolding story lines reveal the climate of the discourse environment in which we conduct our studies. In an institutional setting complete stories are rarely told; further, there are ownership rights:

certain people are allowed to tell certain tales (Boje 1991). Stories change depending on the positions of the stakeholders who tell them. The unfolding institutional story line creates a shared construction or "history" through which participants can find meaning in past events, the present moment, and an anticipated future.

Yet the storied nature of the cultures we study is as ephemeral as the passing of clouds. Storms blow in, and in the blink of an eye, they disperse on the wind. What is left is our memory of the trees lashing against the windows and an ancient need to tell about how awe inspiring or, perhaps, frightening it had been. God willing, someone is there to listen—to help make sense of it all.

> It is not history one is faced with, nor biography, but a confusion of histories, a swarm of biographies. There is order in it all of some sort, but it is the order of a squall or a street market: nothing metrical. It is necessary, then to be satisfied with swirls, confluxions, and inconstant connections; clouds collecting, clouds dispersing . . . What we can construct, if we keep notes and survive, are hindsight accounts of the connectedness of things that seem to have happened: pieced together patternings, after the fact. (Geertz 1995, 2)

In our fieldwork, it is easy to be distracted by all the movement, but I have found the stories endure. If we stick around and listen, stories hold it all together and carry us forward.

My use of narrative in this study was an attempt, as Stephen Crites so beautifully describes, to hear the "sacred stories"—stories that celebrate the powers on which our existence depends, stories that orient our lives and establish the reality of our world. From my perspective, these are stories of healing and the holy life force that moves through a garden. Crites states that sacred stories can never be directly told; they lie too deep in the consciousness of a people. However, "these stories live, so to speak, in the arms, and legs, and bellies of the *celebrants*" (1971, 295, italics added). This is the call of phenomenology that I hear: to bear witness to the embodiment of this knowledge. My attention to stories was to capture the moving forms that "carry the authority of scripture for the people who understand their own stories in relation to them" (1971, 295). I have witnessed "the arms, legs, and bellies" of children as they celebrate their primal connection to the earth. Can you imagine a science that carries such *authority*? A science with ascent to theory, yet grounded in the phenomenological *mundus*. It is in these "most significant mundane stories"(1971, 296) that we attempt to articulate the sacred. Here then is the "sacred science" Peter Reason (1993) calls for in response to the secularized, standardized, bland, ugliness of contemporary social science. From this perspective, my purpose became clear; I was here to record these mundane stories, to inscribe these holy texts for others to read and interpret.

validity criteria, getting it right.

The stories we write, in other words, are judged not just as narratives, but as nonfictions. We construct them knowing that scholars will evaluate their accuracy, and knowing too that many other people and communities—those who have a present stake in the way the past is described—will also judge the fairness and truth of what we say. Because our readers have the skill to know what is *not* in a text as well as what is in it, we cannot afford to be arbitrary in deciding whether a fact does or does not belong in our stories. Someone among our readers—a bemused colleague, an angry partisan, a wounded victim—will eventually inform us of our failings. Nature, of course, will not bother to construct such a critique, but plenty of others will step forward to speak on its behalf as we ourselves have done. We therefore struggle to anticipate criticisms, to absorb contradictory accounts, and to fit our narratives to what we already know about our subject. Criticism can sometimes do more harm than good—sapping the life from a story, burying strong arguments beneath nitpicking caveats, reinforcing conventional wisdom at the expense of new radical insights, and murdering passion—but it can also keep us honest by forcing us to confront contradictory evidence and counternarratives. We tell stories *with* each other, and *against* each other in order to *speak* to each other. (Cronin 1992, 1373–74)

As I begin to anticipate these and many other criticisms of the experimental text I seek to create, I wrestle with the appropriate criteria to judge the validity of this story. How will you and I know that I got it right? Lincoln (2001, 25) states that at the most fundamental level, validity asks, "What is it about this inquiry which would render it transparently faithful enough to enable me to act upon its findings?" Further, Lincoln suggests that we consider validity as property of both the products and the processes of interpretivist work. It is no longer enough to judge only the final product as some sort of virginal birth, the result of immaculate conception. Those of us who dwell in the terrain of alternative paradigm inquiry (critical, feminist, participatory, action research, and the like) must look for signs all along the way that our work is good, useful, and authentic. What follows are the signposts and processes I employed to judge the goodness of this study.

Catalytic Validity. Here research is judged by the "degree to which the research process reorients, focuses, and energizes participants" (Lather 1986, 67). Catalytic validity is evident in the ability of our research participants to better know and transform their circumstances. Similarly, Norman Denzin suggests the authenticity of interpretive ethnography be judged by its "truth effects" (1999, 514). In other words, are you moved to action? introspection? discourse? tears? anger? Lincoln (2001) clearly underscores this point stating that research reports that fail to engage readers or prompt action have failed the catalytic criterion. You, dear reader, will judge the validity of this work by the resonance you *feel in your body*. I want my audience to not only know this story in their heads but also feel it in their bodies. Laurel Richardson (1998) calls this "kinetic" validity and suggests our texts should inspire something beyond themselves. We have dwelt in the *disembodied* stratosphere of the mind for too long now. As Richardson (1997, 167) queries, "How valid can the knowledge of a floating head be?"

Triangulation. The authenticity of constructivist inquiry is reinforced by seeking multiple data sources, methods of data collection, and theoretical schemes (Lincoln and Guba 1985; Lather 1986). Triangulation provides the research community with a sort of 3-D vision of reality. Taking Gregory Bateson's (1982) idea of binocular vision one dimension further, triangulation delivers a depth of understanding not found from either a single or dual perspective. What becomes of utmost importance with triangulation is the acuity that arises out of *difference*. Differing perspectives when integrated, sharpen our vision, creating depth perception. Lather (1986) underscores this point, that triangulation functions in research to seek "counterpatterns" as well as convergences. Teachers who tell me they simply don't have time for the garden, the students who tell me they think the garden is a dumb idea, the administrator who only sees the garden as a means for improved student assessment scores, all counterpatterns that contribute to the validity of this inquiry.

Reflexivity. Laurel Richardson (1999) includes "reflexivity" in her set of new criteria for evaluating creative analytical practices (autoethnography, messy texts, performance, poetry, drama, and the like) in ethnography. As a standard for evaluating quality, Richardson explains that in "writing-stories" (narrative about the context in which our writing is produced— which this text very much is, at one level) we offer critical reflexivity about our self in different contexts as a valuable analytical practice. This reflexivity situates writing in other parts of one's life such as disciplinary constraints, social movements, familial ties, and personal history and longings. With this added dimension, new questions about the relationship between writer and subject are surfaced and granted room to breath. Persistent reflexivity indicates how our "working theories" have been changed by the logic of the data gathered along the way.

Aesthetic Merit. When I first stumbled on this criteria in Laurel Richardson's work, I began pondering what this might mean in the aesthetic void of dissertation writing. Richardson (1999, 666) asks, "Does this piece succeed aesthetically? Does the use of creative analytical practices open up the text, invite interpretive responses? Is the text artistically shaped, satisfying, complex, and not boring?" These questions align with Peter Reason's vision of human inquiry that has as its purpose both truth *and* beauty:

> But it seems to me central to a worthwhile epistemology that its knowing is beautiful. What is the warrant for your knowing? is the traditional epistemological question. To my mind one sound answer might be, It is beautiful, or It leads to a beautiful life. (Reason 1993, 279)

Citing James Hillman, Peter Reason further clarifies our understanding of beauty in knowledge construction not simply as adornment but as "the essential condition of creation as manifestation" (1981, 28). I interpret this to mean that the creation of our inquiry and the ordered arrangements of our fieldwork should pull us in—into the aesthetic depths and beyond the superficiality of surfaces. Denzin and Lincoln (2000, 1061) affirm that as we move into this "seventh moment" of qualitative research, the telling of the tale—the representation—becomes the art. This art is now expressed in myriad *beautiful* forms. The clinical and colorless still life born of traditional research reporting is no longer the only legitimate rendering. These one-dimensional studies of measurement and proportion have reached the limits of their use. Like the great impressionist painters of the nineteenth century who broke free from the limitation of realism, we now have license to represent the world with blurred lines and pastel hues. As we assess the quality of postmodern ethnography, the question then becomes, Is it beautiful?

Understanding.   Finally, and perhaps most important, I take the criteria of "understanding" from Harry Wolcott. Wolcott describes that in understanding, he seeks "a quality that points to identifying critical elements and wringing plausible interpretations from them" (1994, 366). Yet he cautions that there is never a single, exact set of circumstances with a "correct" interpretation. Similarly, Richardson (1999) asks if our work contributes to an understanding of social life from a grounded or "embedded" perspective. She expects that our understanding should be embodied in our texts. In other words, "good" qualitative work should demonstrate an understanding of this grounded experience to the reader. Schwandt (1999) further clarifies that the quality of our understanding is accomplished not by a masterful standing over an object or by adherence to strict methodological prescriptions for analysis but rather by dwelling in that relational space between familiarity and strangeness *where things can go wrong*. And so getting it right means entering into our research projects fully open to the possibility that it could all go wrong. Central to Schwandt's thesis is the idea that getting it right has more to do with the *conditions* of our conversations—our relation to the world—than with the outcome. Wolcott's and Schwandt's words reassure me as I attempt to remain open to the confounding nature of fieldwork. I know I am "getting it right" as I watch my preconceived notions of various outcomes dissolve into the cold, hard reality of an "underperforming" school. I am on the path of understanding as I loosen the reins of "my research" and begin to follow the teachers and students where they need to go.

Catalytic validity, triangulation, reflexivity, aesthetic merit, and understanding, these are the delicate threads that hold it all together, allowing me to drive away from school each day feeling at peace with myself and my work. These are the standards of goodness that signal I am getting it right, for the time being anyway. Simultaneously, as a qualitative researcher, I am historically situated in the throes of the great validity debate. I watch as validity gives way to trustworthiness, which gives way to authenticity, which more than likely is just another placeholder. One can only speculate on what comes next. But ah, what a welcome relief. Doubts about validity and reliability in my previous work are what brought me to qualitative inquiry. And I think it was Harry Wolcott's writing that encouraged me to stay. The evening I read Wolcott's stunning essay entitled "The Absurdity of Validity," I cried. I cried because I had never heard a researcher talk with such honesty and candor about "what really matters":

> For my personal health, safety and sanity, this time more than ever I need to get things as "right" as possible, and I feel a certain urgency about it. I do not compartmentalize my personal and professional lives: I personalize the world I research and professionalize the world of my experience . . . I can state unequivocally that I find no counsel or direction in questions prompted by a concern for validity. There is no exact set of circumstances here, no single and "correct" interpretation, nothing scientific to measure that tells us anything important. For every actor in these events there are multiple meanings. In spite of seemingly direct access, I have never been able to sort out even my own thoughts and feelings . . . I do not have conclusions to present. I try to understand, rather than to convince. (Wolcott 1994, 356–68)

This time, more than ever, I, too, need to get it right. Like Harry, I need it for reasons of health and sanity. For as Wendell Berry so wisely muses when queried about his motivation for writing: "I am attempting a life not a career." Words to live by. Just about sums it all up. In this convergence of grief and garden, research and writing, self and other, art and science, private and professional, I am, above all else, attempting a life.

the write-up.

The form this ethnographic interpretation has taken could not have been accurately predicted or methodologically prescribed, for this task of getting "their" lives into "our" works (Geertz 1988) is never a straightforward endeavor. However, for the sake of a little cognitive economy, I will call my cumulative write-up (or is it writing down?) a case study, though I'm not sure how much meaning that construction holds these days. I suppose this category is useful in as much as it will set this text apart from conventional scientific reporting. What I do know is that I count myself among this "new generation" of ethnographers who are more concerned with telling local stories than with making some contribution to a monolithic master narrative (Bochner and Ellis 1999). And I think this concept of telling a story should not be underrated or misunderstood. As ethnographers, we have a responsibility to hold the question, How are things going to unfold here? Without pushing for an answer, the story then actually becomes a mystery—much like life. This mysterious quality has made my work more engaged, and I think more engaging for the reader. It closes down a whole set of worries—the what-ifs—and opens up an infinite set of possibilities. Storytelling as case reporting text deserves one additional clarification: that is, our stories are reliable constructions of reality or vehicles for truth (Bruner 1990; White 1981; Ricouer 1984). Clifford Geertz (1988), with his extraordinary wisdom and way with words, condemns the commonly held perception that "reality has an idiom in which it prefers to be described," and that if literalism is lost, so is fact.

I think it is safe to say that somewhere in our schooling, the hegemony of "factual" science began to erode the intrinsic value of stories. We have begun to fear that stories are embellished half-truths, or worse, to cease to believe the storyteller's message at all. Rather, we place our faith in the techno-scientific world where reality is summarized in ten-second sound bites of black and white. We are swimming, no, drowning in data—decontextualized, value-free, meaningless data. This "antinarrative narrative" threatens to overwhelm the last vestiges of continuity or meaning in our lives (Sandlos 1998). Stephen Crites emphatically suggests that when we give up the story, we give up a *condition* for moral human existence. "Ethical authority, which is always a function of a common narrative coherence of life, is overthrown by a naked show of force exercised in the name of reason or in the name of glandular vitality" (1971, 311). Nonetheless, I think there survives, deep in our cultural memory, a need to shape our experience into a meaningful story. As ethnographers, storytelling is our strength; our "tales of the field" hold the promise of a new story for our children and their future on planet Earth.

CHAPTER NINE

Telling the story
all the way through.

Who is now to be persuaded? And of what?

—Clifford Geertz, *Works and Lives*

Time to wrap things up, pull it all together. Author Dorothy Allison says, telling a story all the way through is an act of love. A colleague asks me, "Are you going to close with the story about Soup From Our Stoop?" "No, I don't think so." I hear myself reply. Sure it's a good story—a community-wide event, soup from the garden, Alice Waters corn chowder, those gorgeous kid-made pottery bowls, two thousand dollars raised for our local food bank, the media coverage—but that wouldn't see this story all the way through. The soup story is too easy, too comforting, might leave the impression they all lived happily ever after. Soup From Our Stoop might've been a shooting star, and I continually ask myself, What endures? My editor asks, "What do you have in store for the last chapter?" I tell her I am unsure just yet. She suggests access to nature and whole food as an issue of social justice might be the thread that connects. Sure, yes, that will be there, couldn't be otherwise. But the vehicle for this message must come from the kids, has to be authentic; give me just a few more days with the kids. It will come. And so we gardened, and I waited for the story to find me.

A few weeks passed and one evening the phone rang; it was Kristan. Neither of us are phone people so I knew whatever her message, it was important. "Laurie, I've got to tell you about Thomas. He's become absolutely engrossed in the garden; you know the signs: the worms, the digging, seeds in the pockets, rooting through the compost," she recited all the familiar symptoms we both knew by heart, like doctors consulting on a diagnosis. "Only this time there's a twist. For the past three days he's been carting a little tomato plant back and forth to school. When I unloaded him off the bus this morning, sure enough, there it was again, you know, a transplant cut out from one of those plastic cell packs of six. Every day he brings it

into the room, puts it on the grow cart, and takes it home at night. He's hauling that plant back and forth, home to school, home to school; it is killing me. Oh, and he wants you to help him transplant it to a bigger pot when you come in tomorrow," she paused, "because it's going with him to Georgia." "He's moving back!?" I yelped; my heart tore wide open. "Yup, he's going back to live with his mom," she replied. "I guess Dad can't support him anymore."

> **to·tem** \tōt-əm\ *n*,
> **1 a :** an object (as an animal or plant) serving as the emblem
> of a family or clan and often as a reminder of its ancestry
> —*Merriam-Webster's Collegiate Dictionary*, 10th ed.

You need to know this broken bird, this child of poverty has seen more suffering in his short nine years than most will ever see in forty-nine. Brought to us a year ago, this fragile spirit immediately fell into the ranks of the at-risk children at Jonesville School. An angry child, Thomas spent most of the year closed off to the world. Sadly, the state's educational agenda for fourth graders fails to account for the great overriding life forces of grief, pain, hate, loneliness, rejection, hunger, fear, or hopelessness. Weaned too soon and yanked from his nest, this fledgling had nothing firm to hold on to. No true North. No guideposts, not even a map.

Until, praise be, the pull of the earth. Working the warm spring soil, Thomas found his one true home and grabbed on for dear life. I know the moment it happened, Friday, May 14, 2004, our big garden day. I had recruited my brood of university students to help. There were flats of transplants (tomatoes included), packets of seed, rakes, hoes, shovels, stakes, and string. We could finally get the garden in after a long, hard winter.

We worked like crazy fools, starved for the soil as we all were. The garden got planted, yes indeed. In that warm frenzy of souls and soil, during that annual spring ritual of renewal, Mother Earth took hold of Thomas and he in turn held on for dear life. And in that clearing, She made him a promise, a promise to nurture and sustain him the rest of his days.

> Nature in all her vast diversity will nurture and sustain you,
> and me,
> and the ruby-throated hummer feeding outside my window.
> If only,
> we will remember, once again,
> what it is to dwell in the place where we live.
> The things of the world will come and go.
> But a ripe tomato
> in the hot August sun—summer in the palm of your hand,
> is always the color of love.
> And that,
> I have found
> is one thing that endures.

telling the story all the way through.

As I write this final chapter, we are planning and preparing for our fourth season in the garden. We have received external funding from numerous sources totaling close to fifteen thousand dollars—a king's ransom by Jonesville School standards. Red ripe strawberries are being harvested from our raised beds, and English shelling peas hang heavy on the vine. I am

> Why do we garden?
> to make the world pretty
> and it looks pretty and so
> Animals and peple can servive

nursing a wicked blister from pushing a tiller to prepare the soil for our forty-by-fifty-foot greenhouse to be constructed this summer. Hardly seems fair to talk of challenges, but the following are the bumps and twists I see up the road a piece. No happily-ever-afters. No comfort text.

I was fortunate to have landed in a school rich with experienced, creative teachers who were able to see the potential of the garden and run with it. Seven of those teachers are gone. All but one of my dearest gardening colleagues and key informants are gone. Gone owing to attrition, layoffs, early retirement, and enticing offers to "get out of the classroom." Our urban schools are tough places to teach; they are a revolving door to children *and* teachers alike. Although the garden provided these teachers with a place for creative teaching and learning, a sense of community and all the other claims made in the previous chapters, the pull of the earth lost this tug-of-war being fought in our urban, underperforming schools. This is a huge loss. In many ways, we are starting over from scratch. So many new teachers with no understanding of the garden represents a steep learning curve and yet another large investment of my time. I wonder how many times will this cycle repeat itself. Will I be able to sustain the continuity of leadership for the garden in the years to come? Is it naive to expect teacher ownership of the garden in this pressure cooker of public schooling?

Curricular demands continue to loom large—a constant threat to any creative endeavor or attempt to break out of the restrictions imposed by mandated assessment. Apologizing for this predicament, Betty explained, "We are sworn to teach the state curriculum; every teacher takes an oath." The continuing challenge will be to frame the garden as a relief from mandates—a place to creatively integrate across the curriculum, not as one more thing to teach in their overscheduled days. Unfortunately, I am told that very few new teachers entering the profession understand how to integrate the four core areas of the curriculum into a meaningful whole. Kristan, in her usual candor, once articulated what I dared not, "The garden is very upsetting to me." Upsetting because we are torn. Torn between what we know is good and right for the children, for ourselves, for the environment, and for education, and yet knowing full well what is rewarded in the system. The structure of the system reinforces and rewards compartmentalized academic gains, not whole person or whole community development. She concluded, "In an attempt to prove things to the state that we cannot prove, we have to be dedicated to the pacing guide." The garden is upsetting because we have witnessed its potential and yet we may simply run out of time.

As I write this closing chapter, it is tempting, if not realistic, to say we *have* run out of time. In the four years I have been at Jonesville School, I have seen classroom time dedicated to assessment quadruple. At many schools in this district, well over twelve weeks of the school year are dedicated to some form of standardized performance assessment. A key informant rattles off the list of assessment acronyms for me and soon runs out of fingers to count the number of tests she must administer. Teachers are now held accountable at the national, state, and district level for student success. I do not write this to enter into the great assessment debate; rather, I raise this as a competing demand on teachers' time. No Child Left Behind is not going away any time soon, nor is the assessment associated with this policy. I wonder what it is we lose as a society when seemingly everything in a child's day is in service of the test.

We are challenged by time and we are challenged to *prove* the garden's worth. "Proof" takes more time than our institutionalized systems of education are willing to give—a catch-22. A terribly clever means of control, the official pace has outstripped our ability to make meaning, thereby silencing any discourse for change. Authentic assessment of any academic gains associated with garden activities will take more than the one year of study I was officially granted. I have no earthshaking numbers to report to policy makers and administrators pounding the table for academic improvements. As suggested by the teachers, a rubric was developed for evaluating academic gains as a result of the garden activities; however, with a half dozen other assessments being administered, I don't have the heart to push for yet another. Perhaps I should? Further complicating any authentic assessment of the garden is the extremely high mobility of the population we serve at Jonesville School. This is the "revolving door" commonly associated with the face of poverty. "Flight" from the school often cycles according to three-month eviction notices. My dear, dear Jason was pulled out of school in December—gone. Thomas is on his way back to Georgia. Darrell, Timmy, Anthony—gone. It is difficult to measure academic gains when you live life on the run, though somehow this seems not quite the metric we should be pursuing, does it? How do we connect this next generation to Mother Earth when theirs is a life that will not give them the time or place to make contact? How close to the pain do we go? How do we break the cycle of poverty to give these kids a chance? These are the questions that plague me. Carol hopes to see a "difference in investment in the garden" with her returning students next year. She hopes to witness a "progression in their connection to the earth." If Carol can remain hopeful at the end of the day, then we all have an obligation to sustain this hope; this is the least we can offer in a world of hopelessness.

In casting a critical eye to the project, I feel impending threats on my time and ability to give the children and teachers of Jonesville School the support they need. There is no getting around it; participatory research takes time, more time than the machinations of academia will usually tolerate. Time, my time, is what the teachers have requested as they become engaged in this project. The teachers do not want or need more lesson plans, worksheets, guidebooks, or curricula; they yearn for deep lasting relationships in the classroom and across those borders into community and into our colleges and universities. Participatory research extends this hand of commitment. Yet once again we are torn. Everywhere I look, I see the strain of doing too much and moving too fast. Like my old washing machine so easily thrown off balance by the spin cycle, we are tossed about by this worn-out machine of public education. Slow down, pull the plug, make it stop. Give us time. Change the reward structure, measure what matters.

what endures?

One evening while working through a peer debriefing session for this study, I struggled aloud with the nomenclature of this summative placeholder we call "conclusions." Wasn't this exactly what I should resist? This heavy burden of concluding seemed incongruous with the complex, messy, conflicted, fluid context of my research. As John Horgan (1996) muses in *The End of Science*, ". . . things get more and more complicated, they don't converge to a single point. They spread out and disperse in a very complex way . . . firm beliefs dwindle, doubts multiply." Ian Stronach and Maggie MacLure "trouble" their "closing" chapter by setting in motion the idea of "opening" and "closure" as interrelated, "not separate, not independent of each other in their ability to do their work, not dialectically related so much as mutually and reflexively self-constituting and self-subverting at the same time" (1997, 148). Even as I write this "closing" chapter, I remain "open" to the cold, hard reality that "getting lost" is inevitable. And yet wise old Clifford Geertz says that as we traverse from "being there" to "being here" we must find somewhere to stand, at least for the time being. This is precisely what my colleague asked of me that evening: "Laurie, what are five things on which you can stand?" So here goes, a solid place for the time being.

1. We know that culture is in part molded by the characteristics of the environment. Add a garden to a school environment and, sure enough, the culture changes. A living garden is a potent force in reshaping school culture. The Jonesville School garden catalyzed cultural transformation, symbolizing and sustaining hope, growth, and community. "Underperforming school" no longer holds the cultural identity it once had for Jonesville School.

2. As teachers and children continue to experience loss of time, loss of control, and loss of place in their lives, a garden is a powerful leverage point to reverse these losses. For a very small investment of space and money, the garden has provided a venue for healing these wounds of modernity. The larger rhythms present in our little thirty-by-thirty-foot plot of earth cannot be segmented, fragmented, or disconnected. You cannot hurry Mother Nature, nor should you hurry a child. The garden is a portal to a slower, richer experience of life, vastly different from the clipped pace of public education.

3. The garden connects children to the organizing principle of experience. Our children are starved for experience. They are sending us signals as they only know how, they wiggle, they squirm, they "act out," and tragically, we medicate. In the garden, children experience comfort, security, belonging, pleasure, and wonder. But there is more to this; Matthew Fox (Sheldrake and Fox 1996, italics added) says, "Our souls shriveled up during the Cartesian era because *we have been cut off from experience*, cut off from the earth, the animals, plants, rain, sun and stars. *We have shrunk our souls, whereas we are all here to become great souls.*" In the garden our souls expand.

4. A plot of soil with a packet of seeds can become an important place of self-expression. We are all trying to create ourselves, to become uniquely alive, and tending the earth ignites our creative life force—though I have known this all my life—this finding truly caught me off guard. Mother Earth allowed teachers and students to feel more present in their work, in their schooling, and in their personal lives.

5. Finally, the garden allows us to change the status of food for all involved. When one gardens, food can no longer be viewed as a mere commodity for consumption. Fast food, which has a pernicious hold on our culture, cannot compete with the red-ripe strawberries outside our cafeteria doors. But my message is not simply the value of fresh food alone. Somewhere at the intersection of food, fire, and feminine instincts, something sacred happens. At this nexus, we are brought into the ritual of communal goodness that leaves one nourished in body and spirit.

This is where I stand, for the time being.

a few recommendations.

As a participatory researcher, the lines between recommendations for practice and recommendations for research are blurred. Where one begins and the other ends is not clear. And, much like conclusions, I'm a bit uneasy these days with this business of recommending anything to anyone. However, having said that, I wouldn't mind changing the world; so in the spirit of making the world a better place, here are a few insights worth pondering.

1. Open yourself to emergent design. Emergent research, emergent planning, emergent process, emergent teaching, emergent learning, emergent anything. Go ahead; let it unfold. I promise, you won't be disappointed. By remaining open to the unknown, we allow space for people to engage with their most pressing issues. It is liberating. Let go the reins of control and listen; you can't imagine what you'll hear, what you'll learn, and most important what you'll do.

2. While you are there, stay awhile. Stay a long while. You'll be tempted to leave, but don't. Stay with the process and remember it takes time. Hang with it; we are complex, tangled, contradictory

beings. The pay is atrocious and the hours are long but stay with it. You will be rewarded, this I promise. You'll turn the corner and never look back. Prolonged engagement pays dividends in currency rarely traded these days: care, commitment, and human understanding. Good stuff this is. Slow down, it is worth the wait. Make a commitment and draw near to the people and place where you live. Again, ask yourself, "Where am I going to declare my loyalty? Where am I going to exercise my citizenship?"

3. While you're waiting, be sure to reflect. Reflect out loud so we all can hear. I mean it. Our closed system of discourse needs to reflexively come clean regarding our politics, ethics, ways of knowing, and other entanglements that occur in *all* research and teaching situations. Reflexivity acknowledges my vulnerability as an author, and I like that because I am tired of the smooth, shiny certainty found in our academic journals. Who are we kidding? The older I get, the less certain I am about anything; though I'm darn sure I don't want to go it alone. As I begin to value and express my uncertainty and ignorance about where my research is going and what my findings mean, I have gained a spaciousness in which new possibilities can expand and grow.

4. We hold the power of legitimized knowledge production in academia; make something happen. Don't become complacent with your privilege. Jonesville School has leveraged my academic affiliation to gain district recognition, garner funding, attract media attention, and deflect further scrutiny. Go ahead, you pick. There are hundreds of untold stories out there waiting to be heard; grab the spotlight, then step out of the way. Vice versa for schools and teachers: demand reciprocity, collegiality, and meaningful results from the researchers who walk into your world.

5. Find your passion or your pain and there is your research. Don't do it any other way. What is it the poet Rumi says? "You must stay up all night and circle round your life." You'll be tempted to go the well-worn path of convenience, proximity, brevity, run the stats, publish or perish; but don't do it. Take time. Listen deeply. Find your calling. In making that "one, hard choice" to follow my pain, I lost my self and found my lifework.

6. Finally, one last recommendation on behalf of Mother Earth. Do not attempt to codify the garden. The real magic of the garden cannot be planned, codified, packaged, scheduled, or aligned with standards, guidelines, benchmarks, or curricula. Don't try to put

wonder in a box. It doesn't work. Remember, the garden is magic because it doesn't look like, smell like, taste like, behave like school. Nature is wild, unruly, smelly, fecund, messy, unpredictable. Give her some space and go "plan in the doorway."

epilogue.

There is a knot in my stomach this morning, which reminds me of the many difficult good-byes I've known in my life. Death and birth, two sides of the same coin, no matter, both hurt like hell. I am a daughter writing myself through grief. I am a woman writing myself into being. I stand here in the driveway not wanting to leave; the engine is running. It is time to go. Toot the horn, roll down the window; did they see you wave? Throw a kiss. Where did the time go? As I back down the driveway and pull away, the pages of the memory book fly out the window caught on the winds of tomorrow. I must travel on faith now, but my frail faith is battered and dented, hardly a comfort. The needle on the compass spins. It is dizzying this life. But I am here to tell you that as sure as spring follows winter, the tears dry, your head clears, and there, off in the distance, is an opening. It'll be there I promise. Just when you are about to conclude that all is nonsense, the universe will throw you a lifeline.

References

Barthes, R. 1981. *Camera lucida: Reflections on photography.* New York: Hill & Wang.

Bateson, G. 1982. Difference, double description, and the interactive designation of the self. In *Studies in symbolism and cultural communication,* ed. F. Allan Hanson. Lawrence, Kans.: Univ. of Kansas Publications in Anthropology.

Behar, R. 1993. *Translated woman: Crossing the border with Esperanza's story.* Boston: Beacon Press.

———. 1996. *The vulnerable observer: Anthropology that breaks your heart.* Boston: Beacon Press.

———. 1999. Ethnography: Cherishing our second-fiddle genre. *Journal of Contemporary Ethnography* 28 (5): 472–84.

Bellah, R. 1985. *Habits of the heart.* New York: Harper & Row.

Berry, W. 2000. A conversation with Wendell Berry. *Image: A Journal of the Arts and Religion* 26: 45–56.

———. W. 2001. The idea of a local economy. *Orion* 20 (1): 28–37.

Blanchot, M. 1986. *The writing of the disaster.* Trans. A. Smock. Lincoln: Univ. of Nebraska Press.

Bochner, A., and C. Ellis. 1999. Which way to turn? *Journal of Contemporary Ethnography* 28 (5): 485–99.

Bohm, D. 1996. *On dialogue.* London: Routledge.

Boje, D. 1991. The storytelling organization: A study of story performance in an office-supply firm. *Administrative Science Quarterly* 36: 106–126.

Bruner, J. 1990. *Acts of meaning.* Cambridge, Mass.: Harvard Univ. Press.

———. 1991. The narrative construction of reality. *Critical Inquiry* 18: 1–21.

Crites, S. 1971. The narrative quality of experience. *Journal of the American Academy of Religion* 39: 291–311.

Cronin, W. 1992. A place for stories: Nature, history and narrative. *The Journal of American History* 78 (4): 1347–76.

Deleuze, G., and F. Guattari. 1983. *On the line*. Trans. J. Johnson. New York: Semiotext(e).

Denzin, N. 1999. Interpretive ethnography for the next century. *Journal of Contemporary Ethnography* 28 (5): 510–19.

Denzin, N., and Y. Lincoln, eds. 1998. *The landscape of qualitative research*. Thousand Oaks, Calif.: Sage.

———. 2000. *Handbook of qualitative research*. Thousand Oaks, Calif.: Sage.

DeVault, M. 1996. Talking back to sociology: Distinctive contributions of feminist methodology. *Annual Review of Sociology* 22: 29–50.

Duncan, D. 1998. Four Henry stories. *Orion* 17 (2): 24–33.

———. 2000. Man of two minds. *Sierra* 85 (5): 52–57.

Eisner, E. 2002. The kind of schools we need. *Phi Delta Kappan* 83 (8): 576–83.

Esteva, G. 1994. Re-embedding food in agriculture. *Culture and Agriculture* 48: 2–13.

Fox, M. 1995. *Wrestling with the prophets*. San Francisco: Harper San Francisco.

Frank, A. 1995. *The wounded storyteller*. Chicago: Univ. of Chicago Press.

Geertz, C. 1988. *Works and lives: The anthropologist as author*. Stanford, Calif.: Stanford Univ. Press.

———. 1995. *After the fact*. Cambridge, Mass.: Harvard Univ. Press.

Gergen, K. 1988. If persons are texts. In *Hermeneutics and psychological theory*, eds. S. B. Messer, L. A. Sass, and R. L. Woolfolk, 43–51. New Brunswick, N.J.: Rutgers Univ. Press.

Goodman, N. 1980. Twisted tales; or story, study, and symphony. *Critical Inquiry* 7: 103–19.

Gould, S. 1991. Enchanted evening. *Natural History*, (September): 4–14.

Guba, E., and Y. Lincoln. 1998. Competing paradigms in qualitative research. In *The landscape of qualitative research*, eds. N. Denzin and Y. Lincoln, 195–218. Thousand Oaks, Calif.: Sage.

Harper, D. 1987. *Working knowledge*. Berkeley: Univ. of California Press.

———. 2000. Reimagining visual methods. In the 2nd ed. of *Handbook of qualitative research*, eds. N. Denzin and Y. Lincoln, 717–30. Thousand Oaks, Calif.: Sage.

Hillman, J. 1981. *The thought of the heart*. Dallas: Spring.

Horgan, J. 1996. *The end of science: Facing the limits of knowledge in the twilight of the scientific age*. Reading, Mass.: Addison-Wesley.

Jackson, J. 1990. "Déjà Entendu": The liminal qualities of anthropological field-notes. *Journal of Contemporary Ethnography* 19 (1): 8–43.

Kahn, P. 1999. *The human relationship with nature*. Cambridge, Mass.: MIT Press.

Lather, P. 1986. Research: Between a rock and a soft place. *Interchange* 17 (4): 63–83.

———. 1993. Fertile obsession: Validity after poststructuralism. *The Sociological Quarterly* 34 (4): 673–93.

———. 2001. Getting lost: Feminist efforts toward a double(d) science. From Politics and ethics in post-foundational times, a symposium conducted at a meeting of the American Educational Research Association, Chicago.

Lincoln, Y. 2001. Varieties of validity. In vol. 16 of *Higher education handbook of theory and research*, ed. J. C. Smart, 25–65. New York: Agathon Press.

Lincoln, Y., and E. Guba. 1985. *Naturalistic inquiry*. Newbury Park, Calif.: Sage.

Manning, P. 1995. The challenges of postmodern ethnography. In *Representation in ethnography*, ed. J. Van Mannen, 245–70. Thousand Oaks, Calif.: Sage.

Marcus, G. 1994. What comes (Just) after "Post"? The case of ethnography. In *Handbook of qualitative research*, eds. N. Denzin and Y. Lincoln, 563–74. Thousand Oaks, Calif.: Sage.

Mattingly, C. 1994. The concept of therapeutic "emplotment." *Social Science and Medicine* 38 (6): 811–22.

Mills, S. 1991. Standing in the places we live. *E Magazine* (September/October): 40–56.

Mishler, E. 1995. Models of narrative analysis: A typology. *Journal of Narrative and Life History* 5 (2): 87–123.

Oliver, M. 2000. *The leaf and the cloud*. Cambridge, Mass.: DaCapo Press.

Palmer, P. 1983. *To know as we are known*. San Francisco: Harper & Row.

Patton, M. 1990. *Qualitative evaluation and research methods*. Newbury Park, Calif.: Sage.

Polkinghorne, D. 1988. *Narrative knowing and the human sciences*. Albany: State Univ. of New York Press.

———. 1991. Narrative and self-concept. *Journal of Narrative and Life History* 1 (2): 135–53.

Quinney, R. 1996. Once my father traveled west to California. In *Composing ethnography: Alternative forms of qualitative writing*, eds. C. Ellis and A. Bochner, 357–82. Walnut Creek, Calif.: AltaMira Press.

Reason, P. 1993. Reflections on sacred experience and sacred science. *Journal of Management Inquiry* 2 (3): 273–83.

Reinharz, Shulamit. 1979. *On becoming a social scientist*. San Francisco: Jossey-Bass.

Richardson, L. 1994. Writing as inquiry. In *Handbook of qualitative research*, eds. N. Denzin and Y. Lincoln, 516–27. Thousand Oaks, Calif.: Sage.

———. 1997. *Fields of play*. New Brunswick, N.J.: Rutgers Univ. Press.

———. 1998. Fiction and ethnography: A conversation. *Qualitative Inquiry* 4 (3): 328–36.

———. 1999. Feathers in our cap. *Journal of Contemporary Ethnography* 28 (6): 660–68.

Ricouer, P. 1984. *Time and narrative.* Chicago: Univ. of Chicago Press.

Rowan, J. 1981. In *Human inquiry: A sourcebook of new paradigm research,* eds. P. Reason and J. Rowan. New York: J. Wiley.

Sandlos, J. 1998. The storied curriculum: Oral narrative, ethics, and environmental education. *Journal of Environmental Education* 30 (1): 5–9.

Schwandt, T. 1999. On understanding understanding. *Qualitative Inquiry* 5 (4): 451–64.

Sheldrake, R., and M. Fox. 1996. *Natural grace: Dialogues on science and spirituality.* London: Bloomsbury.

Shepard, P. 1977. Place in American culture. *The North American Review* (fall): 22–32.

St. Pierre, E. A. 1997. Methodology in the fold and the irruption of transgressive data. *Qualitative Studies in Education* 10 (2): 175–89.

Stronach, I., and M. MacLure. 1997. *Educational research undone: The postmodern embrace.* Buckingham, U.K.; Philadelphia: Open Univ. Press.

Swimme, B. 1996. *The hidden heart of cosmos: Humanity and the new story.* New York: Orbis.

Toulmin, S. 1982. *The return to cosmology: Postmodern science and the theology of nature.* Berkeley: Univ. of California Press.

White, H. 1981. The value of narrativity in the representation of reality. In *On narrative,* ed. W. J. Mitchell, 1–24. Chicago: Univ. of Chicago Press.

Williams, Terry Tempest. 2001. *Red: Passion and patience in the Desert.* New York: Pantheon Books.

Wolcott, H. 1994. *Transforming qualitative data: Description, analysis, and interpretation.* Thousand Oaks, Calif.: Sage.

About the Authors

Laurie Thorp

Laurie Thorp is director of the Residential Initiative on the Study of the Environment at Michigan State University. In this role, Thorp has the unique privilege of bringing together students from five colleges to study and engage with pressing environmental issues. Thorp also serves as faculty advisor to the MSU Student Organic Farm, a fifty-member Community Supported Agriculture (CSA) farm and source of the best carrots you've ever tasted. Thorp is currently working to bring more local, organic, and fairly traded food to the university food system. She also tends the earth in her own backyard with her husband Joe and their two felines.

Kristan Small

Kristan Small has taught elementary school for fifteen years and is involved in empowering children to create a meaningful curriculum for themselves through gardening and composting. Small is an organic gardener and a weekend potter, in addition to raising earthwise children.

Daniel Brooks

Daniel Brooks was born two days before the end of the seventies (the disco era had luckily petered out by the time he became cognizant), the youngest of four and the son of a tall, nearly bald man who spent forty years teaching just outside of Detroit and a woman who spent fifteen years teaching elementary education down the street. Brooks is a graduate of MSU with a degree in Philosophy, Peace, and Justice. Don't ask him what it means to earn a degree in Peace and Justice; and definitely don't ask him what it means to earn one in Philosophy. He owes you a drink if you have a good idea on what to do next with his life.